The pages of this hope-filled bo
encounters with Jesus Christ,
profound principles of truth th
Like stone steps on a transform
step by step ahead of the reader, leading to purpose in our pain.

**Kevin Shepherd**, *CEO Crossroads Christian Communications Inc. & YES TV*

David and I have known Paul Willoughby for over 40 years, many of those years as he was directly involved with Crossroads/*100 Huntley Street/Nite Lite Live*. His compassionate heart for hurting people is evident in all he does, and in particular, in the writing of his book, *Don't Waste Your Pain — The Journey from Brokenness to Wholeness*. Packed with encouraging stories of God's tender intervention in the midst of difficult circumstances, this is a book you will find hard to put down. I highly recommend it!

**Norma-Jean Mainse**, *First Senior Producer, 100 Huntley Street and Wife of late David Mainse*

What a great read with so many insights by Paul Willoughby whose own life is so revealing and inspiring at the same time. He overcame pain and suffering and now shares how so many others have too, for all of us to learn from. From Justin Bieber's mother to all the wonderful scripture quotations, Paul's book is so meaningful, real and helpful with God as the centrepiece.

**Jerry Howarth**, *Toronto Blue Jays radio broadcaster 1982 through 2017*

You will be inspired and impacted by "Don't Waste Your Pain." Its message comes directly from the life and experiences of its messenger, Paul Willoughby. He provides a realistic portrayal of the pain that he and others have experienced. He skillfully illustrates how the "God of all comfort" has transformed that pain into a deeper grace and knowledge of God which enables one "to comfort those in any trouble with the comfort we ourselves receive from God" (2 Corinthians 1:3-5).

**David Wells**, *General Superintendent, Pentecostal Assemblies of Canada*

Paul Willoughby's personal transparency and compelling story-telling ability make *Don't Waste Your Pain* a powerfully heart-moving, faith-building book. Pain is the universal human experience, but there is hope because of the One who was wounded so that we might find wholeness. Let this book chart the way for you.

**Dr. James Bradford**, *Lead Pastor, Central Assembly of God, Springfield, MO*

Inevitably, all of us on our human journey experience pain. Paul Willoughby in *Don't Waste Your Pain*, is not being flippant, but is pointing us in a direction we tend to avoid. The point, which he makes so well, is don't lose those lessons which can be learned from our pain. This readable and practical take on an age-old issue is a beautiful opening for us all, to walk through a door of eternal learning.

    **Brian C Stiller**, *Global Ambassador, The World Evangelical Alliance*

I'm surprised that a book about pain is so readable. Paul Willoughby has filled these pages with personal stories, stories of friends, stories from home and abroad, and stories from the Bible to share with us the rich biblical truth that our pain isn't wasted. Not a drop of it. The Lord Jesus is not afraid of hard questions. He overflows with hopeful answers, and you'll discover many of them here.

    **Robert J. Morgan**, *Bible teacher and author*

In *"Don't Waste Your Pain,"* Paul Willoughby takes the reader along an important biblical path to discovering God's plan uniquely for them, no matter the circumstances. His gentle style is soothing for any reader, capturing the unspeakable travails of those featured in his book; and the impacting message that one is not sentenced to woundedness forever, for there is practical healing, freedom, and purpose. Paul Willoughby's own childhood trauma combined with his gift of empathy is striking early on. He captures the readers trust as he testifies of the nurturing Hand and miraculous, transformative power of God.

    **Christine D-Williams**, *award-winning broadcast journalist, and best-selling author*

In Paul Willoughby's book, the release of pain is found in the courage of storytelling. Experiences often hidden from even ourselves are shared in the discovery that pain recognition begins within the healing of profound listening. We find new resources woven in the hope that Christ's humanity knows our need of divine accompaniment.

    **Christine MacMillan**, *Commissioner and Founding Director, The Salvation Army International Social Justice Commission. United Nations: Multi Faith Advisory Council member*

I am so thankful that my dear friend Paul finally wrote this book; because in its pages you will discover that the God of Scripture has more than enough food and drink for exhausted, discouraged, depressed and hungry souls. Paul, in his own inimitable style, demonstrates how God still transforms moments of depression, trauma and abuse, into moments of refreshment, peace, hope and joy.

    **Dr. Corville E. Peters**, *Producer/Host AT THE CROSS Live*

Life can be filled with ups and downs, pain as well as triumph. Learning how to overcome its pain and challenges can be difficult. If you are struggling to make sense of your hurts, or how to overcome your past, I believe this book can help you. Paul doesn't offer unproven theories or wishful clichés, but shares from his own personal experiences of abuse and brokenness and how Jesus set him free. This book also includes insights from the lives of men and women of the Bible whom God delivered and used powerfully, and documents the personal stories of people who have faced debilitating pain and tragedy and yet through faith in Christ, have overcome. Highly recommended!
    ***Matt Tapley***, *pastor, Lakemount Worship Centre*

Moving, enlightening, and uplifting! This book proves that there's life at the end of broken dreams when we allow Jesus to take charge! Turning the pages brought me back into the Nite Lite studio listening to Paul Willoughby taking live telephone calls.
    ***David Lau***, *Marketplace Pastor, Richmond Hill Chinese Christian Church*

This divinely inspired book arrives just as the world enters its second year of the COVID-19 pandemic, a crisis that has caused pain to us all, mentally, emotionally, and even spiritually. Even so, the Bible never promises a pain-free existence. In fact Christ says in John 16:33 that "In the world you will have tribulation; but be of good cheer, I have overcome the world." And that is Paul Willoughby's message: pain **is** real, but Jesus enables us to transcend it, **if** we allow Him into our hearts. This book will show you how.
    ***David Onley***, *former Lieutenant Governor of Ontario, Television Journalist, and Associate Professor at the University of Toronto*

This book and story is long overdue - yet much needed for this time!
    ***Margaret Fishback Powers***, *author of "Footprints"*

In an easy to read book and in a deeply personal way, Paul Willoughby provides hope in the midst of despair. He weaves his own story into the book as he also tells the stories of others who've suffered. And, more importantly, he points the way towards healing by gently incorporating Scriptural principles and teaching. As he says, "ultimately the greatest healing for our pain starts when we allow Jesus to take charge of our lives. If ever there was a book everyone needs to read—not "should" read, but "needs" to read—it is Paul Willoughby's *Don't Waste Your Pain*.
    **Barrie Doyle**, Author of the *Oak Grove Conspiracies* novels and "*Musick for the King*"

# DON'T WASTE YOUR PAIN

*The Journey from
Brokenness to Wholeness*

**DON'T WASTE YOUR PAIN:**
*The Journey from Brokenness to Wholeness*

© 2021 by Paul Willoughby
Published by DREAM Publishing and Design

All rights reserved. Except for brief excerpts for review purposes, no part of this book may be reproduced or used in any form without written permission from the publisher.

All Scripture quotations, unless otherwise noted, are taken from the *Holy Bible, New International Version®. NIV®.* Copyright © 1973, 1978, 1984 by International Bible Society. Used by permission of Zondervan. All rights reserved.

Scripture quotations marked (NLT) are taken from the *New Living Translation* copyright © 1996, 2004, 2007, 2013 by Tyndale House Foundation. Used by permission of Tyndale House Publishers Inc., Carol Stream, Illinois 60188. All rights reserved.

Scripture quotations marked (ESV) are from the *English Standard Version ®*, copyright © 2001 by Crossway Bibles, a publishing ministry of Good News Publishers. Used by permission. All rights reserved.

Scripture quotations marked (CEV) are from the *Contemporary English Version* Copyright © 1991, 1992, 1995 by American Bible Society. Used by Permission.

Scripture quotations marked (MSG) are from *The Message*. Copyright © 1993, 1994, 1995, 1996, 2000, 2001, 2002. Used by permission of NavPress Publishing Group.

Any internet addresses (websites, blogs, etc.) and telephone numbers in this book are offered as a resource to you. While correct at the time of publishing the author cannot verify the accuracy of these resources beyond the date of publication. Websites mentioned do not imply an endorsement by the publisher, nor do we vouch for their contents.

# Dedication

To my darling wife, Gloria:

You are a lover of God and a gifted teacher and communicator of His Word who has stood beside me faithfully these many years, wherever God has taken us. You are the amazing mother of our children, Joel, Jonathan, and Rebecca; a wonderful mother-in-law to Amanda, Vera, and Nathan; and an incredible Nona to Ivy, Lily, Daniel, Paul, Denver, Chloe and Anna. But most of all, you are my loving and beautiful wife. To you I dedicate this book.

# Table of Contents

Acknowledgments .................................................................... 10
Foreword .................................................................................. 11
Chapter 1: Hurting? You're Not Alone ................................ 13
Chapter 2: Healing is Possible ............................................... 23
Chapter 3: Your Past Doesn't Determine Your Future .... 33
Chapter 4: Don't Keep Your Pain Locked up Inside ........ 43
Chapter 5: Our Wounded Healer .......................................... 59
Chapter 6: New Meaning for the Hurts of Life ................. 71
Chapter 7: Equipped Through Brokenness ........................ 81
Chapter 8: God Can Turn Your Life Around! ................... 91
Chapter 9: The Pain of Loss and Shattered Dreams ....... 103
Chapter 10: Forgiveness and Freedom .............................. 117
Chapter 11: Look Beyond Your Own Brokenness .......... 129
Chapter 12: It's Not Too Late ............................................... 141
Chapter 13: Don't Waste Your Pain! .................................. 155
Steps to Healing ..................................................................... 165

# Acknowledgments

To my dear friend and former Associate Producer of *Nite Lite Live*, David Kwan, you encouraged me to write such a book, thank you for believing I had something to say.

David Mainse, one of my heroes, took a risk on a twenty-five-year-old who knew nothing about television yet had a burden to help the broken in the middle of the night. I'm so thankful David had a chance to read the first draft before he passed away and agreed to write the foreword.

I'm deeply grateful to my son Jonathan for his work on this project and seeing it through to completion. Thank you to Cassandra Irving of Resonate Communications Inc. for her help in the genesis of this project, as well as to Jeannette Terrell for her editing assistance. Also to Jim Craig, my very dear friend of many years for his literary assistance and ideas.

To my father and mother, Norm and Ethel Willoughby, and my father-in-law and mother-in-law, Joe and Bessie Grieco, who have touched my life in profound ways, thank you. I am so grateful for your love and encouragement! To Tom Richardson and Daniel Ippolito, thank you for giving me a start in ministry as a young man.

To Robert and Ellen King, dear friends whose generosity enabled me to publish this book, I am so grateful.

To the many others unnamed, my heart is filled with gratitude for your influence in my life.

To Gloria and our children, Joel and Amanda, Jonathan and Vera, Rebecca and Nathan, who always encouraged me to keep going and not give up, thank you! But most of all, my heart is filled with thanks to our Lord Jesus Christ for giving His mercy and grace to me daily.

# Foreword

*(Written before David passed away, after he read the first draft)*

This book is about Paul's lifelong journey to becoming, in my judgment, the most compassionate man I know. For years he hosted a middle-of-the-night, open-line television show. Pattie Mallette, Justin Bieber's mom, was a young mother with much pain in her life when she shared her struggles and faith several times with Paul and other hurting people who could not sleep.

In 1979, I offered Paul the opportunity to host, from our Toronto studios, a late-night telecast such as he had previously hosted from CKWS TV in Kingston, Ontario. He turned me down. I could not understand why. Now, reading his manuscript, I understand for the first time. He writes, "I knew inside that I wasn't ready to host the late-night program yet. Though I couldn't articulate it at the time, somehow I had an inner awareness that I simply had not suffered enough. What could I possibly say at age twenty-seven to people who were going through difficult and traumatic times? How was I to enter into their pain when I had known relatively little myself?" You will discover, as I have, that Paul did enter into the deep pain of others during his years in Idi Amin's Uganda and with India's "untouchables." My wife, Norma-Jean, who worked most closely with Paul in the early years of the nationwide daily telecast *100 Huntley Street*, says of Paul, "The character of Jesus was very evident in Paul's life. His compassion for people in pain was a most unique, godly example to us all."

I'm absolutely confident that this book will challenge and change lives.

**David Mainse**
*Founder and first President Crossroads*
*Christian Communications Inc.*
*Crossroads Television System (CTS)*

*A portion of the sales of this book will go to support initiatives helping the 250 million Dalits in India, as well as education opportunities for orphaned children in Northern Uganda.*

NOTE: At the end of each chapter, you will see a box like the one below, inviting you to go to the official "Don't Waste Your Pain" website for resources, archived footage, and video interviews. If you have a phone or tablet handy, just open the photo app and hold it over the QR code – it will take you to the website instantly where you will find the resources for that chapter.

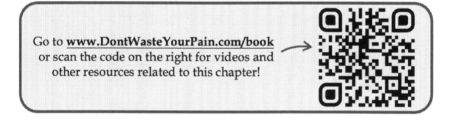

Go to **www.DontWasteYourPain.com/book** or scan the code on the right for videos and other resources related to this chapter!

# Chapter 1: Hurting? You're Not Alone

Over the years God has brought me on a journey of realizing that He can use us despite our brokenness and pain. I'm not sure about you, but I used to think God could only use our strengths and talents. However, as I've journeyed in life I have come to see that God can also use our weaknesses and hurts, if we allow him to. Even though we have painful experiences in life – and we all have them – he can redeem them for His glory.

For many years I was privileged to work alongside David Mainse as the Associate Producer for the Christian television program *100 Huntley Street*. Later I produced and hosted a late-night television show called *Nite Lite Live*. As the name suggests, it was a live call-in talk show in the middle of the night, from 2:00 am to 4:30 am. Many people wonder, "who would be up at that hour?" The truth is that it had one of the highest ratings of any program at that time of night. Why? Because many who were hurting and broken were up at that time. Perhaps sickness was keeping them awake, or a broken relationship made it impossible to rest. For some it was financial pressure that weighed on their minds, while others battled depression, anxiety or fear. Night after night I would have guests share how God transformed their pain and hardship into something beautiful and useful. There were some who would become relatively famous, such as Pattie Mallette (Justin Bieber's mom). Others were sports stars and musicians. Some had been former drug addicts and alcoholics or had come through terrible abuse, but they all shared one thing in common: *the amazing hope and transformation that Jesus can give!* Seeing God change lives in such wonderful ways I've come to believe: **God doesn't waste our pain**! Through the pages of this book you'll hear some of their stories as well as how the Lord took my own experience of pain and used it for his honour. We'll also look at specific truths from God's Word to help us move from *hurt* to *wholeness* to *fruitfulness*.

## You're Not Alone

As we start I want you to know two things: First, *you're not alone*. Second, *there is hope!* While no one has gone through exactly what you have, many others have had deeply painful experiences. Many have journeyed past their pain to a place of hope and freedom – something they once thought would never be possible!

We all have pain. But, it is our choice whether we will run from those experiences, or whether we will allow God to bring healing to our lives, in order that we can pass on that same healing to others. In this way our pain is not wasted.

I remember when I was 18 years old playing football with some friends on a beautiful summer day. Jim was playing quarterback and threw a pass to Larry, who I was defending. Larry caught the pass and turned, and at that moment his muscular shoulder connected with my face – wham! Excruciating pain coursed through my body and I crumpled to the ground, unconscious. They carried me off to the hospital where x-rays showed I had a shattered cheekbone, so bad that it needed reconstructive plastic surgery!

That wasn't the first time I'd broken a bone. As an active boy who loved sports, injuries seemed fairly common. And just as common was what happened after the injury – a trip to the doctor to get it fixed. We didn't try to deal with it ourselves, but took the steps we knew were necessary in order for healing to take place.

Similar to how we deal with physical pain, there are steps that can help us deal with emotional pain, trauma, and abuse. A person with a broken bone doesn't have to stay wounded forever. Neither does someone with a broken heart.

I still have a scar from that football accident, a metal plate in my cheek, and a set of x-rays to prove it! But it does not hurt anymore.

One of the problems with emotional pain, though, is that the memories often continue to hurt deeply, and if they are not dealt with, the feelings of pain can keep resurfacing. What sometimes happens is that instead of opening the wound up to God for healing we tend to run from it, or hide it, or we allow it to eat us up on the inside with anger.

The journey to healing is not easy or quick. Healing takes time. But if we are willing to take the risk and allow God to touch those areas of pain in our lives, not only can we

> **Healing takes time.**

experience healing, but we can watch as he transforms our past into something useful.

## My Experience Of Pain

Although I've been in ministry now for over 40 years, life hasn't always been easy. I learned early on that pain and brokenness were very real and a part of our world.

For me, the abuse began when I was 11 years old. Though my early childhood was quite innocent, when I reached my preteens, an older male sexually abused me on several occasions. This affected me deeply in many ways, although it wasn't until decades later that I was able to fully understand the impact on me emotionally, mentally, and spiritually.

But even early on there was at least one positive outcome: as a result of my own pain, I became sensitive to the pain and hurt that others experienced in this world.

I was about seven years old when I first recall feeling the sensation that I now identify as emotional pain. Strangely enough, it was while I was in our living room watching an episode of the old western television show, *Gunsmoke* with my three older brothers. The program was in black and white during the late 1950s, but in my imagination, I saw it in living color. For some reason, the bad guys in the Wild West didn't like the idea of a Chinese man with pigtails living in their town, so they went to his barbershop and began to rough him up, and then, to my horror, they cut off his pigtails. Suddenly I started crying, feeling this Chinese man's pain, though not fully understanding why. Yet when I cried, my brothers laughed! What was going on? Why was I crying while they were laughing? Did they not feel what he was going through, too? It would take me years to become accustomed to strongly sensing people's pain and to understand how to respond to it.

In high school, I would often be confronted with similar scenarios, only this time it wasn't unfolding on television, but right in front of my eyes. When I was in Grade 10, one such incident occurred in the boys' locker room. Marty and Doug were the tough guys in our class who thought they could take on anyone. No one dared go against what they said. Unfortunately, they saw the smallest guy in our class Billy, as an easy take, and they continually made life difficult for him. This particular day Marty and Doug were at it again, but instead of sticking to the usual verbal onslaught, they advanced to pushing and hitting Billy. I was no hero and considerably smaller than the two bullies, but something happened inside of me.

"Enough is enough!" I shouted. With other classmates looking on, I grabbed Marty by his shirt, pushed him up against the wall, and yelled, "Leave Billy alone!"

"Who made you a cop?" Marty responded.

"I did," I shot back.

"And what are ya gonna do if I don't?"

"You'll find out."

The whole time this exchange was going on I had Marty by his T-shirt. I was scared to death because both Marty and Doug could have easily walloped me if they had ganged up on me, but they didn't. Amazingly, they complied, and that was the last time they picked on Billy, at least in my sight. Furthermore, from that point on, Marty and Doug became my friends. Maybe no one had ever stood up to them before, I don't know. But something had been working inside of me for quite some time regarding Billy, the little underdog, and I had felt it was time to stand up. I didn't realize then that God was helping me sense His heart for Billy's hurt. After that experience, Billy was able to go to class with some semblance of peace, and I was challenged to get involved, even if it meant getting hurt—because others were hurting already.

Those are my two earliest experiences with the sufferings of others. In the years to come, God would begin to open my understanding of pain in its various forms.

## Margaret's Story

Margaret Davidson was well into her sixties when I first met her before our program *Nite Lite Live* went to air.[1] She was so full of joy and love that it was hard to believe she had endured years of horrendous suffering.

Margaret didn't have any good memories from her early formative years. Although Margaret's mother *told* her she loved her and put food on the table, emotional expressions of love were absent from her mother's heart; there was no hugging or other tokens of affection. Unknown to Margaret at that time was the full reality of her mother's own pain. Margaret's father was an alcoholic and never there to provide, so the entire responsibility of raising the family fell to her mother. Abandoned by her father and emotionally walled off from her mother, Margaret never fully experienced love within her family.

When Margaret was four years old, her older brother started to sexually abuse her. Every Saturday morning like clockwork, Margaret's father would come home to take her mother grocery shopping. Watching this unfold, her sixteen-year-old brother would wait outside until they were gone, then sneak back into the house where he would physically and sexually abuse her. Often the pain and torment was so great that she wished she would die.

Once Willie was finished, he would give her a nickel or a dime and tell her to go buy some candy, which she did, in hope that it would somehow relieve her pain.

It was terrible. Every single weekend, this unimaginable trauma was perpetrated on Margaret. Although she did not understand at the time what sexual abuse was, she did know that what her brother was doing to her was wrong. However, Willie threatened that if she ever told anyone what he did, he would beat her to death, making sure to kill her slowly. As a result, she lived in constant fear of older boys. She developed a motto that over the years grew into a mindset: "I will hurt others before they ever get a chance to hurt me." As a result, Margaret became deeply bitter, sarcastic, and fought back with others with harsh words.

All this time her mother was unaware of the horrible things happening to her little girl within their own home. The torment continued for over a decade, even after her brother was married.

One day it all came to a head. Margaret was walking with her friend to the grocery store when, to her horror, she saw her father with another woman. He had always denied that there was another woman in his life, but at that moment as he stood in line at the checkout with a buggy full of groceries, Margaret saw the truth. At home her mother barely had enough food to put on the table, yet here was her father and this woman with a cart full of food. It just wasn't right! As she stood there, all the hurt and rage that had been building up from years of abandonment, rejection, and abuse came to a boil. "Watch this," she said to her friend as she walked determinedly over to her father. "Hi Dad, I'm Margaret" she said matter-of-factly. Caught off guard and knowing he was discovered, he said, "Who are you?" Then he cursed her vehemently and repeated, "I don't even know who you are!" Margaret's motto was, *I'll hurt you before you can hurt me*. So she fired back at him the only way she knew how, with the same rejection and condemnation with which she had been raised: "I hate you, I hate you!" she yelled, then ran out of the store.

It was around this time that Margaret began going to a nearby church, finding it a safe place of escape from all that was going on at home. It was there that she gave her heart to the Lord and soon thereafter had an encounter with the Holy Spirit where she felt His healing and cleansing. Though it was not instantaneous, it was the beginning and motivated her to seek Jesus in a deeper way than ever before. Gratefully, after the summer Margaret turned fourteen Willie never abused her again, but its effects would haunt her for years.

Sometime later Margaret met Bill at her church, who would eventually become her husband. Once she sensed he was really interested in her and they began talking about marriage, Margaret decided she had to let Bill in on her secret. "I've got something to tell you, but once I do, you will not want to marry me." But to her surprise, Bill accepted Margaret with all her baggage; he loved her unconditionally. Sharing the pain helped, but Margaret continued to struggle. After the birth of her son Blake, she started to have suicidal thoughts and wondered things like, *What if my baby boy hurts his sister? What am I going to do with him?* She tried to fight her fears by crying out to the Lord: "Oh God, give me love for this little boy! Give me love for him, and help me to love unlike my mother, who didn't love me. Help me not to be afraid!"

Motherhood was a painful journey for Margaret. After the birth of her second daughter, she crashed emotionally. It was then Margaret realized the only way she could recover from the years of abuse was to find a way to forgive Willie for what he had done—not to condone it, because of course it was horribly wrong, but to let go of the hatred she had against him. Still, it wasn't until Margaret was standing at Willie's graveside a number of years later that she was finally able to say, "Willie, I forgive you." In that moment, she set herself free from the prison of hate, judgment, and retaliation that had controlled her thoughts, feelings, and behavior for so many years. Now, there was forgiveness, love, and rest. She could finally close her eyes and lay her head down and not be afraid. She was finally free from her fears and nightmares.

Forgiveness certainly did not give her amnesia. There are things that Margaret said she could never forget. But if the memories did come to mind, there was love in her heart to guard her from the pain of it all and to seal the healing with inner peace.

For many years Margaret used her past experiences to help bring hope and healing to other victims of abuse. She traveled extensively, speaking and helping others who have suffered from abuse. With the help of her son Blake, Margaret also wrote a book that tells her story in more detail, *Scars Don't Hurt.*[2]

I can assure you, the Lord did not waste Margaret's pain. Because she gave it all to Him and allowed time for the healing process, she could live in freedom. Because she placed her faith in Jesus Christ and asked forgiveness for the sins she committed against others, Margaret was able to offer that same forgiveness to those who sinned against her—including an abusive older brother like Willie.

Why do I share this story? Because I believe that *painful experiences don't have to define who you are.* They don't have to have the last word. The pain of your past need not determine your future. I

> **Painful experiences don't have to define who you are.**

believe with all my heart that the healing and freedom Margaret experienced can be experienced by anyone who is willing to open themselves up to Jesus and allow him to transform it into something useful. *There is hope!*

My prayer is that as you read the stories in this book, that you will find hope to believe that God can give you freedom and a future. These stories show us that, if we allow Him to, God can take the physical, emotional, and spiritual pain in our lives and turn it into gain. I share these stories with you in the hope they will encourage you to persevere through the pain and into the plan that God still has for your life.

# Further Reflection

*"The LORD is close to the brokenhearted;
he rescues those whose spirits are crushed."*
(Psalm 34:18, NLT)

1. Do you think that it's possible to overcome the pain in our lives?

2. Do you feel that there is hope for you?

3. What part of Margaret's story speaks to you most?

4. This is one example of how the Bible describes those who are broken:

    *Scorn has broken my heart and has left me helpless;
    I looked for sympathy, but there was none,
    for comforters, but I found none.* – Psalm 69:20

    Take some time to write a reflection on this verse. Can you relate to how the author felt?

*"There is hope!"*

---

Go to **www.DontWasteYourPain.com/book** or scan the code on the right for videos and other resources related to this chapter!

## Chapter 2: Healing is Possible

I wasn't the only one in my family that had experienced deep hurt. My father had his own understanding of pain as a young boy growing up in rural Canada. Though he seldom spoke of it, what he did say revealed a distant and difficult relationship with his own father, my grandfather. Nothing my father could do was ever good enough and so there were numerous beatings. But it was his father's words that hurt more and pierced deeper than the physical abuse he endured. Often my father was told, "you're not worth even being called a son," and though he could not remember the number of times those words were spoken, he knew their devastating impact. So, at sixteen my father left home for the city of Toronto, Canada, and a new beginning, even as his mother cried begging him not to go.

In the big city he would get his driver's license, begin to drive an ice truck, and along the way learn to smoke and drink like his buddies. One day while delivering ice he came upon two young ladies walking along the side of the road and offered them a ride. One of them was named Ethel, a lovely redhead. Over time a romance developed, and my father became serious with this young lady, asking her to marry him. When she asked how old he was, he responded that he was 24. This seemed okay because she was 27; however, three weeks before they were married she discovered that he was only 18! Despite this, love prevailed and on a beautiful day in June 1944 Norm and Ethel were married. Within two years their first child was born, my brother Bill, and two years later my brother Doug. Driving truck was rough and my dad struggled with smoking. Though he wasn't a believer, this weighed heavy on my dad because he knew it wasn't the best example for his sons. My mom, though, was a strong Christian who loved to sing and praise the Lord and would often bring the boys to church. One night at home little three-year-old Bill began singing "right now, right now let Jesus have your heart right now." My father was convicted and knew he had to change but didn't know how. Shortly afterward when my mom asked my dad if he'd like to go to church for a mid-week service; to her amazement he agreed.

During the service the Pastor asked anyone if they had a prayer request. My dad, a normally quiet man, surprised everyone when he stood to his feet and said, "Pastor, I've tried to quit smoking but haven't been able to, would you pray for me?" Pastor Hugh McAlister responded, "Norm, would you come down to the front of the church, so we could pray over you?" My dad made his way down and soon the Pastor and elders laid their hands on him, praying that he would be set free from his addiction. My dad said he felt such an awareness of the presence of God like he had never known before and was aware something had happened. He went home that night believing his smoking habit had been broken. However, a couple of days later my dad was at work and craving a cigarette. At that time, he had no idea what "spiritual warfare" was, or that there was a battle going on for his soul. He assumed it was all physical. He saw one of his friends and said, "Smitty, could I have a cigarette?" Smitty replied, "I thought you quit that stuff?" To which my dad said, "I thought I did too, but I just have to have a smoke!" Smitty gladly responded and gave my dad the cigarette. Going out back of the warehouse my father lit up, but as he took his first puff of that cigarette he felt like he was going to be sick. He threw the smoke down, stomping it out with his feet. That was the last time my father ever touched a cigarette. Within a few days he was filled with the Holy Spirit, a Biblical encounter that would give him power to serve Jesus and help him to be a truly committed follower of Christ. It would also help him to forgive and deal with some of the hurts of his own past. Because of his experience of

God's power, that set him free from his addiction to smoking, he and my mom enjoyed a growing love for Jesus and each other. As a result, my dad would get up early and spend the first part of his day reading his Bible and praying before heading off to work.

Because of what the Lord was doing in my parents' lives, by the time I was born, I was raised in a loving home - not a perfect home, for there aren't any. A very important part of our family life was church, and truthfully, I cannot recall a time when I did not go to church.

My twin brother John, and I were born on a Sunday morning in Grace Hospital in Toronto. One week later, we were in church alongside our two older brothers and our parents. Yes, church was a very important part of life for my family; however, simply going to church never saved anyone. As I have learned, the defining factor in one's faith is not which building a person goes into, but *whom* a person allows into the 'building' of his or her own heart and life.

Though my early childhood was innocent and full of many pleasant experiences, that changed when I was abused as a preteen. I became angry and confused and entered a period of rebellion, associating with people who had different values from those of my family. No longer did I want to go to church with my parents, although I still *had* to go, because my dad and mom had the final say. But seeds were being planted in my life which, if left unchecked, would take me in a very different direction from the one in which my parents were raising me to go.

I tried to cope with my inner pain by burying the wounds and the memories in fun and activity. Life moved on and, like many Canadian boys in the 1960s, I dreamed of becoming a hockey player. My hero at the time was a strong and tough defenseman for the Toronto Maple Leafs named Tim Horton—though he's better known today for the chain of donut shops he founded than for hockey!

As I grew older, I realized that playing for the Maple Leafs was not a realistic idea. The pressure of the world began to push me down—not in open and obvious ways, but rather, through subtle temptations that, mixed with the pain of my abuse, caused my heart to begin to harden towards God.

But a turning point came in the summer of my fourteenth year. Our family was together at a Christian camp where the "Gospel Sons" – Terry Law and Dennis Bjorgan – were speaking and singing. Back then, CHUM 1050 AM was *the* pop radio station in Toronto. I wanted to show Terry how cool I was and that I knew the top tunes from the CHUM chart. As I was sharing all this impressive knowledge with Terry, he turned to me and said, "Paul, if you knew your Bible as well as you know that CHUM chart, you'd be on fire for God!" His words pierced me, but I wasn't about to give in so easily. That night, I lay on my bed listening to CHUM 1050 when Dad walked in. I was certain he was going to tell me to turn off my music, and I readied myself for World War III. Instead, he walked over and sat down beside my bed. "I've missed you at the altar, Paul. I want you to know that I love you and want God's best for your life." Squeezing my knee, he repeated, "Paul, I want you to know that I love you and want God's best for your life." With that, Dad got up and walked out. In that moment, the walls I'd built up began to collapse. I had expected a fight but had instead received love, mercy, and an invitation to return to the *Father*. The next night at an old-fashioned camp meeting the altar call was given. It didn't matter to me whether anyone was going to the altar; I had to go forward. I surrendered my life to Jesus Christ as my Savior and Lord. It was a pivotal night in my life. A few days later, at that same altar with no one else praying with me as I worshipped the Lord with my hands in the air, I felt God's presence charging through me like an electrical current and I began to speak in a language that I had

> **Ultimately, the greatest healing for our pain starts when we allow Jesus to take charge of our lives.**

never learned. I was baptized in the Holy Spirit, just like my father had been years before.

Though it would take a long time for me to experience true healing from the abuse I had suffered, this was the first pivotal step. Ultimately, the greatest healing for our pain starts when we allow Jesus to take charge of our lives.

We saw in the last chapter the truth that there is hope. The second key we need to realize is that this *hope and healing starts with surrendering our lives to Jesus*.

## Running from God

Let me return to my father's story for a moment. Unknown to any of us, the Lord was working on my grandfather's heart seeking to get his attention and bring changes in his life. By this time Grandma Willoughby was in a nursing home and so Grandad was living alone at the old farmhouse. One night after heading to bed he heard knocking at the door so he got up to see who could possibly be there at that time of night. However, when he opened the door, no one was there. He thought that was odd, but just went back to bed, imagining something he had eaten caused this strange disturbance! Getting back into bed he tried to fall asleep, when once again there was this knocking at the door. Mystified, he got up again and went to the door, only to find no one there. He wondered what could possibly be happening. Was he losing his mind, or was "Someone" trying to speak to him? Refusing to give in to that thought Grandad pulled the bed covers over his head trying to fall asleep and, finally, sleep prevailed. The next morning my grandad went to his place of work, where he cut grass on the shores of Lake Simcoe, Ontario. As he pushed the manual lawn mower, once again he heard the now familiar knocking sound. Throwing his hands in the air he cried out, "I give up Lord, I give up! Please forgive me!" In the stillness of that early morning hour Grandad fell to his knees and made his peace with God. The ordinary, common ground he had walked over so many times before became for him a sanctuary.

The truth is, my grandfather wasn't expecting to meet God in the ordinary – be that his bedroom at night or his workplace on the shore of a lake in the morning. He simply wasn't expecting to meet God at all. Yet God was pursuing him in all his brokenness. Oh, such relentless love!

What ordinary, familiar, even broken place might God surprise us with his presence? Could we find Him in a lonely apartment, at a kitchen sink, or even in a wheelchair? Yes, my grandfather, like Jacob, may have said, "the Lord is in this place, and I was not aware of it" (Genesis 28:16). Why do we so often feel that way? Is it because the ordinary place is just too common and so we think God couldn't possibly be there? Or, is it because we feel we've made too many mistakes in our life? Jacob was running from his brother when God met him. He definitely wasn't expecting to meet God either.

Often, brokenness and pain do that to us. We find ourselves weary and running. Running from the hurt, from the memories, from our past, and even from ourselves.

Actually, a lot of the people that God ended up using in the Bible started out by running from Him, or from their circumstances. Jacob was not the only one: Moses messed up in Egypt and eventually had to flee for his life after he murdered someone. He spent decades as a dropout shepherd, wandering the desert. Imagine how many times he must have dreamt of Egypt and of his old life in the palace! I'm sure he spent years wishing he could do things over, crying on the inside, thinking he'd messed his life up. He probably felt he was too far gone and that God could never use someone like him. Moses, raised as a prince in Egypt, had to come to the end of himself before he could let God use him.

Another example is David who spent years running from Saul. He may have thought, "God, what about your promises? I thought you told me I'd be king?" Imagine his pain and his anger at being unjustly treated. Perhaps he felt that his dreams were falling apart. Then, even after becoming king, he messed up with Bathsheba and crashed back down to a place of brokenness. This time *he* was the one who misused his power, who terrorized an innocent man, taking his life because of his own out-of-control lust. What a mess! Yet, even here, when David humbled himself and ran back to God he received mercy and grace.

Then there's Peter in the New Testament. Falling on his knees, overwhelmed at the miraculous catch of fish, realizing in whose presence he was. What did he say to Jesus? "Go away from me, Lord; I am a sinful man!" (Luke 5:8). How many of us feel like that? "God," we say, "I've messed up too much! You can't use me, you don't want me. No one else does!" So we give up – discouraged and disheartened at our own weaknesses. But we need to know that *broken people are the very people God wants to use*!

Who or what are you running from? My grandfather, full of bitterness and anger because of his own experience with pain, had been running from God for a long time. But he quickly discovered this God he had run from was Jehovah Shammah, *the God who is there* (see Ezekiel 48:35). My grandfather could not keep this experience to himself and quickly made his way home, changed, and travelled to Toronto to tell his son Norman what had happened. However, when Grandad reached our home my father wasn't there as we'd all gone to the same Christian camp for holidays where my life had been changed a few years earlier. So my older brother Bill, who had stayed behind to finish work, drove him down to see us. They reached the camp just

> **Brokenness doesn't have to be the end of your story!**

about service time, so my dad invited his father to the service. As always, there was lots of good gospel singing and preaching, and that night was no exception. When the altar call was given my dad asked his father if he would like to go to the altar with him. Grandad responded in the affirmative, and there for the first time in their lives father and son were walking down a church aisle to an altar for prayer. As they knelt to pray my grandfather began to sob, and turning to my father asked, "son, can you ever forgive me for the way I treated you when you were a boy?" He then began to tell my father what had transpired within the last twenty-four hours and how the Lord had so directly met him, changing his heart and life. My dad reached over to his father, forgave him, and together they hugged and cried in gratitude for God's amazing grace that had so personally touched their lives. Grandad lived for a few more years after his heart had been so profoundly changed. When it came time for him to leave the old farmhouse to go into a nursing home, my father invited him to come to live in a nursing home near him, and so their last years together were better than their first years.

Like my father and grandfather, brokenness doesn't have to be the end of your story! We are all broken in some way, but gratefully, there is hope for each of us. The good news is that we do not have to stay broken. In fact, great beauty can come forth from the depths of brokenness. The question is, what will we do with our brokenness? Will we *hide it*, *hold on* to it – or *hand it over* to Jesus, the only one who can truly bring healing and hope?

In the next chapter, we will look a little more closely at how deeply God is committed to you and to seeing your brokenness healed.

# Further Reflection

*"Come to me, all you who are weary and burdened, and I will give you rest" – Jesus (Matthew 11:28)*

1. Do you feel like you're running from the pain or the memories of the past?

2. Can you think of other people in the Bible that were running from God, or who seemed to have messed up, and yet who God used?

3. What part of my dad's story spoke to you the most? Why?

4. Have you ever encountered God personally by opening your heart and life to Jesus Christ as your Savior and Lord?

*"Hope and healing starts with surrendering to Jesus!"*

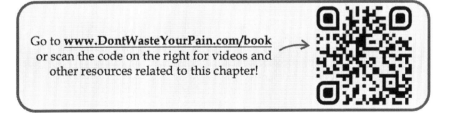

Go to **www.DontWasteYourPain.com/book** or scan the code on the right for videos and other resources related to this chapter!

# Chapter 3: Your Past Doesn't Determine Your Future

Some people think that the heroes of the Bible were perfect people who had it all together. Nothing could be further from the truth! Consider Abraham: he was called the "father of the faithful," yet he deceived Pharaoh by telling him that his wife, Sarah, was his sister (Genesis 12:13,19). On another occasion he told the same lie to King Abimelech. When Abraham doubted God's ability to give him a son through Sarah, he agreed with her plan to sleep with her handmaid Hagar, hoping he could father a child through her (Genesis 16:1–2).

What about Abraham's grandson Jacob, the deceiver, who stole his brother's birthright and his blessing but would later be named Israel or the Prince of God (Genesis 25:19–34; 27:1–41)? And then there's Tamar who engaged in prostitution with her father-in-law, and gave birth to twins who were in the family line of King David, and thus the Messiah (Genesis 38:1–30)? And as we saw in the last chapter, David himself, the King of Israel, became an adulterer and murderer, yet through repentance found forgiveness and restoration (2 Samuel 11:1–27; Psalm 51:1–12). And what of the Apostle Paul, who persecuted the early church and was complicit in the death of Stephen, but became the Apostle to the Gentiles and wrote a significant part of the New Testament (Acts 7:54–8:1)? Yet another example would be Barnabas' cousin John Mark, who deserted Paul on his first missionary journey but ended up writing what is probably the earliest of the four Gospels (Acts 12:12; 13:5, 13).

Sometimes we think, "God could never use me" or "I'm not good enough for God." But we need to remember that the significant failures of these important individuals didn't disqualify them from being used by God.

In fact, *our brokenness is often what brings us to the end of ourselves and to a place where we finally reach out and depend on God.* Consider James 4:6: "But he gives us more grace. That is why Scripture says: 'God opposes the proud but shows favor to the humble.'" When we go through difficult circumstances and are broken, we come to the end of ourselves. We recognize our own weakness, our pride is shattered, and we come to a place of humility. It is in that place of brokenness that God is able to show His favour. The Apostle Paul wrote in 2 Corinthians 12:10, "That is why, for Christ's sake, I delight in weaknesses, in insults, in hardships, in persecutions, in difficulties. For when I am weak, then I am strong." Our personal brokenness does not have to stop us from fulfilling God's wonderful purpose for our lives.

> **Our personal brokenness does not have to stop us from fulfilling God's wonderful purpose for our lives.**

What do we mean by *broken*? Webster's defines it as: "separated into parts or pieces by being hit, damaged, etc.; shattered; violated by transgression; made weak or infirm; subdued completely (as in *broken heart, broken spirit*)."[3]

When we go through difficult times – whether it is the pain of abuse, the pain of loss, physical pain, emotional pain, or something else – it often feels like we have been 'shattered.' We don't have the strength to put ourselves back together, or to pick up all the pieces. This is the place where we need to turn to the only One who can put us back together – the loving God who created us.

After his affair with Bathsheba, David recognized his wrong and repented. He penned the words in a Psalm and cried out, "The sacrifice you desire is a broken spirit. You will not reject a broken and repentant heart, O God" (Psalm 51:17, NLT). God did not reject David, and he will not reject you and me, despite our brokenness.

This is also demonstrated in the life of Jacob. He lied to his father Isaac, cheated his brother Esau, and ended up running away in fear of his life. He finally found work with his uncle Laban, but it wasn't the smooth sailing he'd hoped for. He fell in love with Rachel, Laban's younger daughter, and agreed to work for seven years in order to marry her. But, his uncle tricked Jacob by switching Rachel for her sister, Leah, who became Jacob's wife on his wedding day! After working for Laban for 14 years Jacob fled once more, this time having messed up and still in fear of his brother, he met with God. He wrestled with the angel and came away with a limp – something that would mark him forever. It was a reminder of God's greatness and his own brokenness. But that's not the only thing he came away with, he also left with a new name. Instead of Jacob (which meant 'deceiver'), he was given the name Israel ('one who wrestles with God'). This was to be the name by which his people would forever be called! Every time they spoke that name or thought about their identity, it was a reminder of two things: his weakness, but also his tenacity! Yes, there had been some pain, but he had not given up, he kept on wrestling, he was persistent and determined.

> **His promise for you is greater than your pain;**
> **His destiny for you is greater than the difficulty you've been through!**

The truth is that when we allow God to touch us, even though we may have messed up, or been hurt or sinned against, He can transform us and turn our negative experiences around. He wants to give us a new name. *His promise for you is greater than your pain; His destiny for you is greater than the difficulty you've been through!*

One of the people who can testify to that truth is my friend Maury Blair.

## Child of Woe

Maury is a popular speaker in high schools and prisons. He was my guest on *Nite Lite Live* many times over the years. His traumatic story of child abuse was so disturbing, yet compelling, that viewers began to realize, "if God can help Maury Blair deal with his abuse then maybe he can help me too." As he shared with me, his jovial, fun-loving demeanor betrayed nothing of the horror he had endured as a child. How was this possible?

Maury was born as the result of a summer-long relationship his mother, Alice, had in Michigan, where she had gone to find work. She had truly loved the man, but when she realized she was pregnant, she fled as she did not want to ruin his reputation. However, back in her hometown of Paris, Ontario, people soon started talking when her pregnancy began to show.

Jobs were hard to find; it was even harder for a single pregnant woman. What would she do? How would she survive? She took jobs she would not ordinarily have even considered; desperation causes one to do desperate things.

Then a local man named Cyrus entered the picture. Before she had left for the States, he had expressed interest in Alice and even asked her to marry him, but she had refused. Although she was now pregnant, in a strange way Cyrus still wanted Alice. But he was going to make her pay—her and the child especially. Cyrus and Alice married and had children of their own, but there was no real love between them; it was a relationship borne out of Alice's need to survive, even if her existence was brutal.

Maury never ate with his stepfamily. Instead, he ate whatever food his stepbrothers were able to sneak upstairs to him in their old house. If the old man found out, they would have been in trouble too, but it was Maury who was the primary target of his wrath. Every night Cyrus would come home drunk and stumbled up the stairs. And every night, Maury knew he was coming for him. At first, he had tried to hide, but the old man always found him, and the beatings would be even worse. Cyrus hated Maury intensely and often threatened to kill him. Though Maury's body bore the signs of his stepfather's constant abuse, his spirit bore them even more. Maury saw himself as garbage.

One night stood out in his mind from all the others. His stepfather was filled with explosive anger that seemed to surpass the violent storm that raged outside. As he staggered into Maury's room, he said, "Tonight I'm really going to kill you!" Cyrus opened the window, grabbed Maury by his shirt, and roughly began to lift him up and out of the window. Maury thought to himself, *perhaps I'll finally be free from this pain*. Just as he was about to be thrown down to his death, he heard his mother speak in a commanding voice: "In the name of Jesus, bring that boy in now!" As soon as his mother mentioned the name of Jesus, Cyrus pulled Maury back in and dropped him to the floor. Maury realized that *Someone* must have another purpose for his life. Still, it would be a few years before he fully understood who that *Someone* was.

Reading helped Maury escape into another world. In time, through books on positive thinking and listening to the radio show, *Hour of Decision*, Maury began to understand that God loved him. It was a radical new thought he had never considered before. In time, he gave his life to the Lord Jesus Christ and discovered not religion, but a personal relationship with the God who loved him. As well, he attended the Pentecostal church in their community, where Pastor Jack Ozard took a real interest in him. The process of healing began slowly, and it would take years for Maury to fully forgive his stepfather, but there was no doubt that his life had

> **Your past does not have to determine your future.**

changed. He would then go on to attend Bible College and prepare for ministry.

Maury has helped thousands of young people through Teen Challenge, a faith-based residential alcohol and drug addiction program with centres throughout the world, and his own Breakthrough Ministries.[4] His motto is: "Your past does not have to determine your future." Experts have told him that someone with his childhood traumas would likely have become an imbecile, a convict, a drug addict, a suicide statistic, or an abuser of children. Maury is none of those things. Instead, his life has been used to help other broken people find healing and wholeness through the unconditional love of Jesus Christ. You can read about his experiences in Maury's book *Child of Woe*, or watch the short film of his life, "Child of Woe," available online.[5]

Remember, the heroes of the Bible were not perfect people who had it all together. Despite their failings and mistakes God still used them. This means there is hope for you and me! Our brokenness can bring us to a place of desperation and dependence on God. Our personal brokenness, then, does not have to stop us from fulfilling God's wonderful purpose for our lives. *Rather, it can actually be a pathway for God's power and purpose for our lives.* Brokenness can enable us to fulfill a greater purpose and make us a blessing to many others. Maury learned, as did Jacob and so many other great men and women in the Scriptures: **His destiny for you is greater than the difficulty you've been through!**

## Crying out in Pain

Sometimes we aren't aware of our own need of God until the going gets tough. It was during the difficult times that Israel called out to God, and he answered and delivered them. C. S. Lewis famously said,

> Pain insists upon being attended to. God whispers to us in our pleasures, speaks in our consciences, but shouts in our pain. It is his megaphone to rouse a deaf world.[6]

Some may ask, But why should I call out to God? Why should I believe he has a plan for me? Where was he when I was going through this pain? And more importantly, why didn't he stop it? Where was God when Maury was going through all that difficulty?

You need to know that it's okay to ask those questions. It's okay to be honest with our doubts and ask "Why?" We'll explore this in more depth later, but we need to recognize that God has given us a free will, and people unfortunately use that free will to do evil things to one another.

We also must keep in mind that this world is not just made up of people and God. The Bible also clearly teaches that there is a devil in the mix. Jesus actually called the devil the *"ruler of this world,"* spiritually speaking (John 12:31, NLT; see also John 14:30; 16:11; 2 Corinthians. 4:4). Because of that, the devil is doing all he can to "steal and kill and destroy" people and God's plan for them (see John 10:10). He also influences people towards evil, to do sinful things. The apostle Paul put it like this: *"You used to live in sin, just like the rest of the world, obeying the devil – the commander of the powers in the unseen world. He is the spirit at work in the hearts of those who refuse to obey God"* (Ephesians 2:2 NLT). This doesn't mean we can blame the devil for our actions, "Oh, the devil made me do it!" No, we are each responsible for the choices that we make. But, from a Biblical perspective, we need to realize that the devil is actively trying to influence people towards evil. So it is people, responding to these ungodly impulses, that bring such sin, hurt, and pain into our world.

Why doesn't God stop this? Once again we need to understand that God created us all with *free will*. This means our wills, our hearts, are free to choose to obey God, or obey ungodly desires. God doesn't suddenly stop every evil action that the human heart devises. Think about it for a moment – so many of our every day words and actions are so wicked in His sight, that God would actually have to stop almost everything we do! Pause right now and think about every unkind word you've ever spoken, every selfish deed, every thought that wasn't in line with God's holy standard. If God stopped all sin He would need to stop our thoughts and actions as well. You see, we usually want God to stop everyone else, while at the same time we want Him to let us do what we want!

So rather than put us all in some kind of cosmic straitjacket, God did something else. He put *Himself* in a straitjacket: He came down and was born as a baby in the confines of a body in this sinful world. He did this so that He could experience our pain and offer a way out. A way of redemption. We will look more at how Jesus did this in chapter five.

So where was God when Maury was abused? When others have been abused or mistreated? He is still there, waiting for us to call upon him, to cry out to him, because God has plans and purposes for us greater than we can imagine. Your pain and your past do not negate His plan.

Let's remember the theme of this chapter – your past doesn't have to define your future. No matter how broken you are, the encouraging news is that God can use broken people! In fact, the place of brokenness is often where we see clearest our need for God, the only One who can truly fill our lives with meaning and hope and peace. But we have a choice – will we turn and cry out to him, or will we try to endure the pain on our own?

# Further Reflection

*"For we are God's masterpiece. He has created us anew in Christ Jesus, so we can do the good things he planned for us long ago."*
*(Ephesians 2:10, NLT)*

1. Which biblical figure mentioned in this chapter can you identify with most easily? Why is this the case?

2. What aspects of Maury Blair's story impacted you personally? Why?

3. Do you think God could work powerfully in someone else's life through you? Why or why not? How did Jesus and the apostle Paul look at this issue (Luke 12:11, 12; John 15:5; Philippians 4:13; Romans 8:31, 37)?

4. Do you agree with C. S. Lewis that God shouts to us in our pain? Do you think God has ever tried to teach you anything through the pain you've gone through?

*"Your past does not determine your future!"*

Go to **www.DontWasteYourPain.com/book** or scan the code on the right for videos and other resources related to this chapter!

# Chapter 4: Don't Keep Your Pain Locked Up Inside

One of the most painful situations in my life came at the hands of a fellow Christian. The good news is that just before this season of hardship happened, God introduced me to the woman who would become a true source of help for me through it all – my future wife Gloria.

After high school I attended Central Bible College in Springfield, Missouri. While there I had the privilege of singing, traveling, and recording with the Revivaltime Choir as part of the Assemblies of God's weekly radio program, *Revivaltime*, with evangelist C. M. Ward. Broadcast on over 750 stations worldwide. It was an incredible time of ministry and had a very positive impact on my life.

I remember well a story Dr. Ward shared with the choir about the unusual workings of God in the life of one very broken listener: A man from New York City who had come to the end of his rope and could bear the pain no longer. The man loaded his gun, preparing to kill himself. To cover the sound of the gun, the distraught man turned his radio up to full volume. But just as he lifted the gun to his head, he heard the words, "Put that gun down!" Shaken, the man turned around to see who was interrupting his well-prepared plan. But there was no one there. Suddenly, he realized the voice was coming from the radio. Now the radio preacher had his attention! After Dr. Ward preached, he gave the invitation to come to the "long, long altar." The would-be suicide victim fell to his knees in his apartment and cried out to the loving Saviour of whom Dr. Ward had spoken.

When the program finished, the man found out where the program originated and contacted the staff. Dr. Ward said the incident made him aware of how God could use a message that was prepared days or even weeks in advance to speak to an individual at the very moment of their deepest need.

For me, it was a lesson about how Jesus, because he was willing to take up His own cross, understands our pain, especially that of the most desperate among us. Today as the gospel is shared, He is still working to seek and to save the lost!

I went on tour with the choir in the summer of 1970. Eventually, I made it back home to Toronto to earn some money and prepare for a transition from Central Bible College (CBC) in Missouri to Eastern Pentecostal Bible College in Peterborough, Ontario. It had been a difficult decision because I really enjoyed my time at CBC. But sensing a strong tug from the Lord to make the change I applied, and my transfer was accepted. It was my second year of college. I'll never forget walking into class in Peterborough that first day. I didn't know anyone, but that mattered little: I was immediately smitten by the dark black hair and olive skin of a very beautiful young lady whose name, I would soon discover, was Gloria. Eastern had a student newspaper called *The Illuminator*, and each class was to have two student reporters on its staff. Both Gloria and I were selected to be student reporters for the Communicator Class of '72. It must have been God's providence for, as they say, the rest is history—a wonderful history, indeed.

After Gloria and I graduated from college, we married and began our first ministry experience together that summer as youth pastors at Gloria's home church in Toronto. Revival hit among our youth; dozens committed their lives to the Lord and were baptized in the Holy Spirit. Little did I know how much I would need to remember the Holy Spirit's ministry that summer, for a little over a year later I would be questioning whether God could even use my life in the ministry.

In the fall we returned to CBC in Springfield, Missouri where I finished my final year and graduated with the class I began with, receiving a BA in Bible. The following summer we led a youth team with Ambassadors in Mission (AIM) through eastern Ontario in door-to-door and park evangelism. When the senior pastor of a large Pentecostal church became aware of my involvement with the youth mission team and Revivaltime Choir, he contacted me. After meeting together, he invited me to come on staff as both youth pastor and minister of music.

"But I don't know how to read music!" I said.

The pastor replied, "Paul, you've sung in Revivaltime Choir!"

"I may have sung with Revivaltime, but I've never led a choir in my life, and I don't know how to read music! I'm not sure I'm the person for the job."

He was insistent. "Don't worry, you can do it."

And with that, I was hired. Gloria and I completed our work with AIM and in late August we moved to the city where the church was located to begin our ministry there. It was a great church with a positive history and they welcomed us warmly. However, within the first two weeks of being on staff, I was approached by one of the older men in the church who had a few teenagers in our youth group. He took me out to lunch at a nice restaurant, and I thought, *Wow, is this ever neat! What a nice perk to the ministry.* But as we ate our lunch this man began to tell me what a terrible job I was doing as the youth pastor. As we had only been there a short time I was totally taken by surprise and devastated by what he said. I left the meeting shaken, but I kept it all inside. A few weeks later it was time to try out for the church's ice hockey team. This same man was the coach. Guess who didn't make the team? You're right, the youth pastor. I wasn't Wayne Gretzky or Sidney Crosby, but I could skate and handle the puck decently and I wasn't a bad fourth line player.

Once I learned that I had not made the hockey team, I believed this man was out to get me. I was only twenty-two, and the experience crippled me emotionally. *Fear gripped me.* Literally a crippling fear, so much so that I was not able to function in my areas of responsibility. It was like I was in a straight-jacket emotionally.

What made the situation particularly hard was that the man was old enough to be my father, so I believed what he was saying about me was true. His criticism made me second-guess my worth and calling, undermining the foundation of who I was – a person made in the image of God. If you had seen me in those days, you would have seen 'devaluation' written all over my face. My body language shouted to people, "Don't come near me! I don't like who I am, and you won't either!" I even considered leaving the ministry altogether.

Paul David Tripp, in his book on suffering, highlights how the pain of the past compounds the hurts of the present.

> You and I never come to our suffering empty-handed. We always drag a bag full of experiences, expectations, assumptions, perspectives, desires, intentions, and decisions into our suffering. So our lives are shaped not just by what we suffer but by what we bring to our suffering. What you think about yourself, life, God, and others will profoundly affect the way you think about, interact with, and respond to the difficulty that comes your way.[7]

My past hurt combined with my present pain further damaged the way I viewed myself, leaving me trapped in a web of negativity and despair.

Yet by God's grace I kept going. Gratefully, as mentioned earlier, the year before all of this happened the Lord had given us a major revival among the youth at Gloria's church in Toronto. It had been an extremely positive experience, and many of those same youth were still serving God. I knew God had His hand on my life and I knew therefore that leaving the ministry wasn't the answer, but what was? How would I move past this painful situation?

## Don't Keep The Pain Hidden

One of the things I've learned is that if we keep our pain hidden, it often keeps us from our healing. Think of a physical wound for a moment. If you have a broken bone it may hurt deeply, but what good would it be if you hid it from the doctor? If you kept the pain to yourself? Well, it may heal—but perhaps it would not have set properly. You might be left with a limp or ongoing pain. The best thing you can do is go to a trusted doctor and let them guide you to healing.

In a similar way, we cannot keep our painful experiences to ourselves. There comes a time when we need to bring them out into the open and speak of them. The first step is to pour out our hearts to the Lord. But that isn't all that God wants us to do. There also comes a time when we need to take the second step: to share our pain with a trusted person.

This doesn't mean just telling anyone though! You do not go to a mechanic to fix a broken bone, you go to a trusted doctor. And if you've gone through great trauma, you shouldn't necessarily just share it with anyone. Ask your pastor for the name of a trusted counselor.

It can be painful to share the trauma you've gone through with someone else as it digs up the bad memories, and it hurts all over again. (Just as a doctor checking our wound may actually hurt a little). But in the long run, it opens us up to the possibility of healing.

## Understanding Response Patterns to Pain

In order to move past our pain we need to understand the usual responses that we have when we experience hurt. Unlike a physical injury, *when it comes to emotional pain there is often a level of shame that keeps us from sharing our hurt*. Or sometimes there is the fear of retribution of some kind: if I tell someone what happened, I will be rejected, or I would fear for my safety, or it will impact my finances negatively. And so we keep it hidden.

At other times we fall back on response mechanisms we learned as a child. When we are younger we don't realize that telling the truth about a situation can lead to healing. Or maybe we did share about a painful event and we were mocked or ignored. As a result, we learned to keep things inside.

This is what I often chose to do. As a result of my earlier pain and abuse, my automatic response was to hide it and pretend everything was okay. I had learned it as a response mechanism and didn't tell anyone, not even my wife. Note that this is not a healthy response! If we've been hurt in the past, we should recognize such patterns of behavior. We do this subconsciously, in order to survive, but it will not help us heal.

In my home growing up I'd never learned to share things openly, possibly because my father kept things inside with the same response mechanism to the pain he'd gone through! I never heard him talk about it, and I didn't know how to talk about such things either. (You can see how generations of families can be impacted by these behavioral patterns!)

Counselors often speak of three ways that we respond to painful situations: fight, flight, or freeze! We can either lash out (fight), or run away (flight), or hide (freeze). Being the non-confrontational, people-pleasing type of person, I wouldn't fight or lash out. I recognize now that my response was usually to "freeze". That is, to emotionally withdraw, go into hiding, and not share what I was feeling. It would paralyze me. And when the pain was too great, then my second choice would be "flight." I would move on to another job or role.

Let's look at each of these briefly.

### *Fight*

The "fight" (or "attack") response, is fairly straight-forward. When you are hurt, you lash back out and attack the person who caused you pain. In your hurt and anger, you may also attack others, venting your frustration on innocent people around you. This type of person often becomes very bitter, lonely, and hard for others to be around. In chapter one, Margaret shared how she began to respond in this way to those around her – that is, until Jesus softened her heart!

*Flight*

The "flight" (or "avoidance") response, is where the person runs away from the painful situation. This could be a physical move – for example, a number of times my father left a job and moved to another city when there was conflict at work. This was also one of the common responses I would have to painful situations.

Another, less obvious, form of flight is the use of humour to avoid a painful situation. Now, humour can often be very helpful in reducing stress or deescalating a conflict. But sometimes I would use humour to avoid talking about a painful situation or dealing with an issue. My mother used to say, "if I didn't laugh about it, I'd cry!" So if something touched a nerve, I would make a joke, change the subject and move on—"fleeing" the issue at hand. This reaction, while providing momentary relief from the painful emotions, does not help in bringing about healing.

Yet another form of avoidance is trying to cover up the pain through the use of alcohol, drugs, or substance abuse. But that does not deal with the issue, nor does it help or equip you to deal with future pain. Merely trying to forget your pain will never lead to overcoming it, nor will it bring you to a place of healing. If the stress of life and the pain you feel makes you reach for alcohol to cover things up, that is often a sign that you are not willing to deal with the underlying issues which are causing the problem.

*Freeze*

The "freeze" response paralyzes you in such a way that you feel incapable of functioning. You are so hurt that you are at a loss to know what to do. Your emotions begin to shut down and you feel like quitting everything. You give up on your relationships, your work, even church, and you no longer feel like you are able to keep going any longer.

## The Right Response

Learning a healthy response to painful situations is one of the keys to living a fruitful life. There will always be hurts, wounds, and offenses against us – but how do we respond? Rather than the unhealthy responses of "fight, flight or freeze," we need to learn to "face" the fear or pain that we have been experiencing.

This was brought a little too close to home once, just shortly after Gloria and I were married. We had visited some friends down in Florida and my buddy Dwight asked if I'd go scuba diving with him. "I don't know how!" I protested, to which he replied, "Oh Paul, there's nothing to it! It'll be fun!" (Always be careful when someone says that!) After some fun time snorkeling with our wives on the shallow water side of the reef, Dwight and I took the girls back to shore then headed out by boat to deeper water. Dwight quickly gave me a sixty-second lesson on how to put the gear on, breathe through the regulator and clear my mask. After that, we tumbled backwards into the water, and almost immediately I began to have trouble breathing and clearing my mask. I motioned to Dwight to head to the surface, and there I told him of my challenge. Dwight suggested we once again go underwater and head back to the boat. We attempted this but after a short time when I looked for Dwight he was nowhere to be seen! I turned and turned looking for him, realizing that if I stayed under water it might be the end of me, so I slowly surfaced. My heart sank as I saw how far the undercurrents had pulled me away from the boat. I tried swimming back but the current was too strong. The tanks were getting heavier and heavier and I could no longer keep treading water, so I dropped the tanks, watching them sink into the depths. Feeling a little lighter I tried to stay afloat but at the same time I continued to be pulled farther out to sea. Dwight had reached the boat by this time and started it up.

But he then began to head in a different direction! I was screaming, "Dwight, Dwight," but he couldn't hear me. Dwight headed for another boat for help, but then continued to go further away from me. I shouted and waved but to no avail. Was this how it was going to end, drowned at sea? I could imagine Gloria being widowed after less than two years of marriage!

Finally, after searching for some time the boats turned around to head back to shore. With my life on the line, I cried out to the Lord like never before and at that moment, as the boats were turning around, the sun glinted off something I was wearing and they spotted me! It seemed like forever before they reached me. Dwight pulled me into the boat. I was exhausted, but grateful the ordeal was over!

I did not want to go back into the water for a long time after that! Eventually, however, I realized I had a choice to make: either let fear control me, or *face my fear* and actually learn how to scuba dive properly. So despite some initial hesitation, I resolved to take a proper scuba diving course and eventually became a certified diver. Now, rather than fearing the water, there is freedom – freedom to explore, to adventure, and to enjoy God's beautiful creation. When we choose to face our fears, it can be painful, but also open the door to great freedom!

With that in mind, here are a few steps that will help us *face the pain of our past*, and move into a place of wholeness.

## Steps to Healing

**First**, if there is abuse happening right now, you need to see how you can remove yourself from that situation, even if it is temporary, while you seek assistance. For example, if it is abuse at home, you may need to stay with relatives or someone you trust while you work on dealing with the situation. If it is emotional abuse by a certain group of people, you may need to stop being with them for a period of time. This isn't "flight" in the sense that you are running away from the pain, but you are removing yourself from it, in order that you can deal with it in a healthy way and from a safe distance.

**Second**, we need to cry out to God. He really is on our side, and He can give us the supernatural strength and wisdom to deal with the pain of the past. We also need to *keep going back* to God. Just because we begin bringing our *past* hurts to God (for example, the abuse I had gone through as a child), doesn't mean that there will never be any more pain in the *future*. We still live in a fallen and sinful world. That means we will continue to experience pain in different degrees, and we need God's continual help. But, we don't stop there.

**Third**, we need someone to walk with us through the pain. Often, because we are so wounded, it is hard to be objective and know what steps to take. We need someone else's perspective and wisdom. This was another lesson I learned through my scuba diving incident – we were never made to go it alone. By ourselves there is always the danger that the currents of life will overtake us and overwhelm us. But if we have the support of a trusted friend, if we are able to confide in someone, we find extra strength and encouragement for the journey!

This is where a counselor is so helpful. If you want to talk to a counselor you can ask your pastor or a local church. As mentioned earlier, my wife and I went to "Emerge" ministries for counseling and it was so helpful.[8] If you're not sure of who to call, you can always call Crossroads (the ministry we have been connected with and that started 100 Huntley Street and Nite Lite). They have a 24/7 number you can call for prayer or to be connected to a church or counselor: 1-866-273-4444.

**Fourth**, remember it takes time. We need to understand that our pain has shaped us over time, and it will take time to bring healing as well. Again, just like a physical injury may take months or even years to come to complete healing, so our emotional pain may take longer than we would like it to take.

**Fifth**, take ownership of what we are able to. We need to understand our "raw response." How do we react when we are raw, hurt, or have an emotional wound? Do we resort to any of the "fight, flight, or freeze" responses we looked at earlier? Of course, some things we are unable to change or control (other people's behavior, or the events of the past). But some things you can change: your attitude, your future responses, and even some things about your present situation.

**Sixth**, take small steps. Based on your talks with a counselor, with owning the things that you can control or change, set realistic goals. Do not expect everything to change overnight. But you can be persistent in taking a series of small steps that will help you eventually come to a place of wholeness. Along the way, you may have some struggles – taking two steps forward, a few steps back. But do not give up! Over time you will see and experience change.

I would also encourage you to have a person or a group that you are accountable to. You might not share with them all the details that you'd share with a counselor, but you can share parts of your journey and ask them to help you be accountable regarding the steps you are taking.

**Seventh**, look outward. It is often as we begin to move beyond focusing on our own pain, to the pain of others, that we actually find healing for our own hurts! We'll be talking more about this in the last few chapters of the book.

**Finally**, believe! Keep trusting that God wants your best and can help you.

## The Journey to Healing

The Bible tells us to "pour out our hearts" to God (Psalm 62:8). I did this over and over. But my mistake was that I kept the situation to myself; I did not tell anyone, not even my wife Gloria, what was happening to me. As a result, over the next nine months as youth pastor, I was slowly dying emotionally. At church, when kids were gathered, talking together, I assumed they were talking about me, and I withdrew. Maybe you know that feeling as well? Before choir practice, I would stand behind my closed office door, often weeping, "Lord, I can't go out and do this." But of course, I had to lead the choir so I would dry my tears, put on a good face, and get on with the practice. Though the experience was painful for me, it was probably painful for the choir as well. They knew nothing of what was going on inside me, but they knew I was not myself. I was lacking in self-confidence; the normally jovial and outgoing person I used to be was gone. How different things could have been, had I only shared what I was going through!

Fourteen years later, I met with the senior pastor of that church (who by that time had gone on to assume a leadership position in the denomination), and finally shared with him what had caused me to resign. With tears rolling down his face he asked, "Paul, why didn't you share this with me?" I had not mentioned the disapproving man's name to the senior pastor, yet he knew very well who it was. "During my time there," he continued, "that same man took *me* out to lunch and went up and down both sides of me. If I had not been strong in my own sense of personal self-worth, it would have shaken me, also."

This painful time, so early in my ministry, helped me realize that I needed to change my ways. Instead of keeping things locked inside, I needed to learn to trust the wisdom of Psalm 55:22, which

> **Cast all your cares on Him because He cares for you.**

invites us to "Cast your cares on the Lord and he will sustain you." For emphasis, this is repeated in 1 Peter 5:7: "Cast all your anxiety on him because he cares for you." *Cast* comes from the Greek word *epiripto*, which means, "to throw upon."[9] The word is used in the New Testament here and in Luke 19:35 when people cast their clothes upon a colt Jesus was to ride. God is telling us to literally throw or dump out *all* our cares upon Him when we are struggling.

It also means we should share them with others because he calls each one of us to "carry each other's burdens, and in this way you will fulfill the law of Christ" (Galatians 6:2). Keeping things bottled up inside prevents God and His people from providing the comfort, encouragement, validation, and support that will enable us to get through the painful situations of life. Trapped inside ourselves, only increases our mental and emotional anguish. Today, whenever I see someone struggling to express a difficulty they have walked through, I tell them that they're not alone; all of us have gone through emotional pain. All of us need help. I then encourage them to share their story with a trusted person, painful as it may be, because it is often in the act of pouring their story out that they open themselves up to the sustaining power of God.

Dr. Richard Dobbins, clinical psychologist and founder of Emerge Counseling Ministry in Akron, Ohio, and the Dr. Richard D. Dobbins School of Ministry in Florida often spoke at the District Conference of our denomination. Many times I heard him make this statement: "Until the pain of remaining the same hurts more than the pain of change, people prefer to remain the same."[10] Eventually we realized our need for counseling and both Gloria and I went to Dobbins' Emerge Counseling to help deal with the underlying issues of pain that both of us had gone through over the years. It was not always an easy process, but it helped to look at our struggles with the guidance of a trained counselor. It also allowed us to express our hurts and to learn healthy methods of coping with and responding to painful situations in our lives.

> **Who you are is more important than anything you'll ever do.**

### Who You Are Is More Important Than What You Do

The other thing I learned from this painful experience was the importance of seeking the face of God. The Bible says that "those who look to him are radiant; their faces are never covered with shame" (Psalm 34:5). As I meditated on the Father's face and the radiant look of love, encouragement, and blessing He was giving me, the critical look on the face of the man who hurt me faded, and I was given the strength I needed to stick it out. Prior to leaving that church, Gloria and I went with the senior pastor and his wife to a pastors' conference in Montreal. At one of the services the District Superintendent, Rev. Gordon Upton said, "Who you are is more important than anything you'll ever do." Those words spoke deeply to my spirit about my worth, and as I listened, I wept. As the service concluded I turned and knelt at the pew, continuing to weep, aware that *my value as an individual was far more significant than my performance* as a youth pastor. Those words have continued to speak to me throughout my life and have become the gauge of what is important: my identity as a person made in the image of God.

My early experiences in ministry taught me that, yes, we may have enemies, but God is not one of them! He did not cause my pain or yours; rather, He is the giver of good gifts. James tells us, "Every good and perfect gift is from above, coming down from the Father of the heavenly lights, who does not change like shifting shadows" (James 1:17). The Bible is clear in explaining that not only are we people of inestimable worth, but that God keeps His eye upon us.

### Wounds From Believers

Usually, negative words are spoken by people who have had negative words spoken over them; they just continue the cycle that they themselves experienced. Often they don't even realize the pain they are inflicting. Perhaps because they grew up that way they developed really "tough skin" and are able to easily shrug off criticism, not realizing how it debilitates others. There is truth in the old saying, "hurt people tend to hurt people."

While all painful situations bring great hurt into our lives, sometimes wounds inflicted by fellow believers seem to sting even more. We feel betrayed. If a stranger says something mean we can shrug it off, but if it is a believer or someone we trusted it can cut like a knife.

King David felt this way and wrote:

> *"It is not an enemy who taunts me — I could bear that.*
> *It is not my foes who so arrogantly insult me —*
> *I could have hidden from them.*
> *Instead, it is you — my equal, my companion and close friend.*
> *What good fellowship we once enjoyed*
> *as we walked together to the house of God."*
> (Psalm 55:12-14, NLT)

We need to remember that Jesus was also wounded by one of His closest earthly followers, as well as by those in the general population He came to serve. Sometimes the tendency is to believe them, or to give up in ministry, or to close ourselves off to others completely. We end up never wanting to trust again. But that is not the path of healing. Instead, we should follow the path of Jesus – the wounded healer.

# Further Reflection

*"Give all your worries and cares to God, for he cares about you."*
*(1 Peter 5:7, NLT)*

1. Have you ever been devastated by the critical comments of others? Did it change the way you looked at yourself? How?

2. Did you share your pain with a friend? With God? What was the result?

3. What does God have to say to broken people? (See Psalm 34:8-10, 17-19 and Psalm 46:1)?

4. What part of my own story spoke to you the most? Why?

*"Don't keep your pain to yourself!"*

Go to **www.DontWasteYourPain.com/book** or scan the code on the right for videos and other resources related to this chapter!

## Chapter 5: Our Wounded Healer

After I resigned from my position a new door opened for me as the pastor of a small church in a rural town. I'll never forget how it all fell into place. In my last year at Bible College, I had begun to pray about where Gloria and I should go after graduation. In prayer, the Lord began to impress on me the name of a town called Tweed. It was a rural community of 1,800 people on the shores of Stoco Lake in eastern Ontario. I knew that this town existed, but that was about all. Still, I had a growing sense of Tweed's significance. Gloria suggested we write to the town clerk and find out more about it, so we did. I also wrote the District Superintendent of our denomination and shared my burden with him. He graciously wrote back and said that there was a pastor there currently, but if anything should change, he would contact me. Then we heard nothing more.

Fast forward two years when I was on staff as Youth and Music Pastor of the church where the older gentleman took me for lunch. It was then I attended an annual youth convention. With permission from my senior pastor, I approached the new District Superintendent, Reverend Gordon Upton, asking if I could speak with him. "Might it be about Tweed?" he asked. This took me totally by surprise! Reverend Upton explained that when he took over the position, he had gone through all the files and came upon my letter. Tweed was now looking for a pastor. Would I be willing to let my name stand? God's providence had prepared me two years before for this moment, knowing all along the pain I would go through, yet also preparing a place of refuge for me. Of course, I said yes!

Tweed was a fresh start for us. The wonderful people of that small congregation who welcomed us in July 1974 provided Gloria and me with a place of refuge and healing. This was a season of growth in our lives. At my first Sunday-night service I preached on the soon coming of Jesus, and two people came to the Lord! One was a young man in his early twenties and the other was an older woman. She had formerly been the secretary of the church but had wandered away from God and become involved with another man. It was a great night of victory. After the service was over, I left the front of the church sanctuary and walked into our kitchen where the church parsonage attached to the main building. Suddenly, I sensed a dark, evil presence so thick it could have been cut with a knife. I did not want to alarm my wife, so I said nothing. However, as I climbed into bed that night Gloria said, "Do you feel what I feel?" I said, "Yes, Satan is not happy with what happened tonight." We would find out later that the young man who had come to the Lord had been involved in the occult. I said to Gloria, "Let's pray." I took her hand and said, "Satan, in the name of Jesus Christ, I command you to take your evil presence and get out of here and never return!" Immediately, the evil presence was broken. The intimidator had tried to use fear to bind our young lives and make us ineffective on our very first Sunday of ministry in our new church. What a thief he is! If we let him, he will walk all over us. But Jesus wants us to understand this important truth: "You, dear children, are from God and have overcome them, because the one who is in you is greater than the one who is in the world" (1 John 4:4).

## The Vision

So, began our ministry in Tweed. New people started to come to the church and to the Lord as we reached out to the community. We did not realize at the time how special this season of new beginnings would be, when God would give me a vision for late-night television ministry that would unfold during my second year as pastor at Tweed Pentecostal Church.

Gloria and I were preparing to dedicate our first child, Joel, to the Lord, as well as to be ordained to full-time Christian ministry on the same Sunday. He was the first child born into a pastor's family in the Tweed church in many years, so it was a time of great rejoicing. All that week, I sensed in my heart the need to be alone with the Lord in prayer and fasting to prepare myself for that important day. So I cleared my schedule a little and set aside the thirty-six hours prior to Sunday to be alone with the Lord. It is truly amazing what God will show us if we give him a few hours of our time.

Perhaps I need to say a note about how the Lord would lead or direct me. Some people are "thinkers" and the Lord guides them by implanting thoughts and ideas in their minds as to what He wants them to do. Others are "feelers" who are led by God through what they sense or feel in their hearts. I'm definitely in the second group! While it does not happen all the time, there have certainly been a number of occasions where I would "feel" or "sense" the Lord speaking to me in some way. This time it was not in an audible voice, but through a feeling in my heart, a dream, or just a "sense" that something was about to happen. You will see this come up a few times in the book, especially at crucial moments in my life. This does not mean that I am some kind of saint (just ask my wife!) but it does reflect a reality which the Bible talks about – that God actually does want to lead and guide us by His Holy Spirit.

This was one of those special moments when I felt God impressing something on my heart, and in response I took the time to set aside a few days to focus on the Lord. As I did, a couple of Scriptures began to jump out at me during this time of prayer. One was Isaiah 54:2: "Enlarge the place of your tent, stretch your tent curtains wide, do not hold back; lengthen your cords, strengthen your stakes." The other was, "Go, and proclaim these words toward the north, and say, 'Return'" (Jeremiah 3:12, ESV). As soon as I read those words I instinctively knew that for me they referred to Canada, because in our national anthem, "O,

Canada," we call our country "the true north, strong and free." But what did the Lord want to say to me about returning, about Canada and about lengthening my cords and strengthening my stakes? It was a mystery.

The night after being given those Scripture verses, I had to travel about one hundred miles away to Gananoque, Ontario, to lead a regional youth rally for our churches. Afterward, I headed back toward Tweed driving up Highway 41 from Napanee, Ontario. Around 11:30 p.m., I remember seeing lights and televisions on in the homes of people all along the road. Suddenly, I began to weep as the Holy Spirit spoke to my heart about a late-night television program that would stand as an alternative to viewing the garbage that was on the air. Unable to continue driving I pulled the car over, took out a pen, and began to write down these thoughts, along with the name *Alive Now!* It was some time before I regained my composure and resumed driving. When I arrived home, Gloria was already asleep in bed, so I waited until the next morning to tell her what had happened. That day, we dedicated Joel to the Lord as planned and the District Superintendent, Rev. Gordon Upton prayed over Gloria and me, confirming our ordination into full-time ministry. The presence and power of the Lord was so real in that place! With the vision for *"Alive Now!"* hidden in our hearts, our son newly dedicated and ordination complete, tears flowed freely. Humbly, we were conscious of God's hand upon our lives.

We were both amazed at how the Lord had been working. Just a year and a half before I was a young broken youth pastor who wondered if he should even continue working in the ministry. Now, not only was I the pastor of a church, but also God was giving me a vision to reach out on a national level through a nightly Christian television program. I learned that when a posture of humility grows out of our brokenness and we say, "I cannot put myself together, Jesus; I need you to do that," then the Lord, who is Himself the *wounded healer,* helps us respond to painful situations in a redemptive way.

## Our Wounded Healer

I like to speak of Jesus as our "Wounded Healer."[11] As a result of being wounded on the cross, He understands our wounds. The amazing thing is that because of His wounds He is able to bring healing to us. It is a wonderful paradox. Let us take a look at the first part of this idea – He understands the pain we go through.

This is expressed in Isaiah 42:3: "A bruised reed he will not break, and a smouldering wick he will not snuff out." He deals with us tenderly because He was broken, too. He will not handle us in a rough way. We are safe with Him. The second chapter of Hebrews states,

> But we do see Jesus, who was made lower than the angels for a little while, now crowned with glory and honor because he suffered death, so that by the grace of God he might taste death for everyone. In bringing many sons and daughters to glory, it was fitting that God, for whom and through whom everything exists, should make the pioneer of their salvation perfect through what he suffered (Hebrews 2:9–10).

Jesus brought us salvation through what He suffered on the cross. He was bruised and broken on our behalf. Isaiah 53:5 tells us: "But he was pierced for our transgressions, he was crushed for our iniquities; the punishment that brought us peace was on him, and by his wounds we are healed." This is what enabled Him to become our "Wounded Healer." Jesus is full of mercy and compassion. Rather than being far from us when we are hurting, as some might mistakenly think, He is "close to the brokenhearted and saves those who are crushed in spirit" (Psalm 34:18). God is much closer to you than you may think. And what's more, He is for you! Nothing can stop Him from believing in you and using all things for your good. As Paul declares: "What, then, shall we say in response to these things? If God is for us, who can be against us?" (Romans 8:31).

Amazingly, even though He was God in the flesh, Jesus did not run away from pain. As Philip Yancey says,

> The fact that Jesus came to earth where he suffered and died does not remove pain from our lives. But it does show that God did not sit idly by and watch us suffer in isolation. God became one of us. Thus, in Jesus, God gives us an up-close and personal look at the divine response to human suffering...The record of Jesus' life on earth should forever answer the question, How does God feel about our pain? In reply, God did not give us words or theories on the problem of pain. God gave us himself. A philosophy may explain difficult things, but has no power to change them. The gospel, the story of Jesus' life, promises change.[12]

Jesus knew what it was like to be a refugee, to work hard, to have no earthly father, to have family members that did not believe in Him. And, of course, to be rejected by the very people He came to save, to be mocked and beaten and tortured. To die an agonizing death. But because of His suffering Jesus was able to bring redemption. *His pain was the pathway of healing* for us all. As Peter says, "by His wounds we are healed" (1 Peter 2:24). Peter was there when Jesus experienced those wounds. And in fact, he contributed to Jesus' pain by betraying him. But even then Jesus forgave, Jesus loved, and Jesus reinstated Peter. Peter was able to move on in life without fear or guilt; he could forgive himself as he received the forgiveness of Jesus (see John 21:14-19). That same freedom and forgiveness is available for you, as well!

The Bible is clear that Jesus transforms our lives through His sacrificial death for our sin and brokenness. In John 14:6, Jesus says, "I am the way and the truth and the life. No one comes to the Father except through me." The writer of the book of Hebrews explained the importance of Jesus' humanity to His sacrificial death for us this way:

> Since the children have flesh and blood, he too shared in their humanity so that by his death he might break the power of him who holds the power of death—that is, the devil—and free those who all their lives were held in slavery by their fear of death...For this reason he had to be made like them, fully human in every way, in order that he might become a merciful and faithful high priest in service to God, and that he might make atonement for the sins of the people. Because he himself suffered when he was tempted, he is able to help those who are being tempted. (Hebrews 2:14-18)

Jesus had to become a complete human being in every way like us, except for sin. This qualified Him to serve as our substitute, a human being giving His life for the sins of other human beings. And what is it that qualified Him to serve as our faithful High Priest who could understand our brokenness, even as He redeemed it? The book of Hebrews says, "Although He was a Son, he learned obedience from what he *suffered* and, once made perfect, he became the source of eternal salvation for all who obey him..." (Hebrews 5:8-10, emphasis mine). Jesus' suffering prepared Him to be our Savior, the One qualified to die for our eternal salvation. Even with the Son of God, who never sinned in His life, suffering had to come before He could be the ultimate blessing to all humankind. This suffering equipped Him not only to be the Savior, but also to be our merciful and compassionate High Priest, since He understands the needs of all those who have experienced brokenness in their lives.

Dr. Richard Dobbins, whose teaching has helped me a great deal over the past thirty years, comments on this verse. He states,

> Pain and suffering are unavoidable, so the spiritually and mentally wise person develops a redemptive attitude toward life's normal pain. He

learns not to let what happened in the past steal the enjoyment of life in the present and future. Be aware of what you are saying to yourself during the painful times of your life. In Romans chapter 8, Paul lists a number of painful adversities, and then asks his readers this piercing question: "What shall we then say to these things?" It is what you say to the things that happen to you which is more important than the things that happen to you. Paul answered the question with, "If God be for us, who then can be against us" (see Romans 8:31).[13]

Yes, God is for you! However, you need to be for you, too! Solomon spoke some wise words in Proverb 18:21: "The tongue has the power of life and death, and those who love it will eat its fruit." I really like *The Message* translation of this verse: "Words kill, words give life; they're either poison or fruit—you choose." We do have a choice to speak words of life or death over ourselves and others daily. We have the power to interpret the hurtful things of life for our benefit or for our own destruction. This is true even of the events of our past. Once we come to know the Lord's incredible love for us and His unshakable commitment to us and to our good, we can declare with Paul:

> **What you say to the things that happen to you is more important than the things that happen to you.**

> [31] What, then, shall we say in response to these things? If God is for us, who can be against us? [32] He who did not spare his own Son, but gave him up for us all—how will he not also, along with him, graciously give us all things? [33] Who will bring any

charge against those whom God has chosen? It is God who justifies. ³⁴ Who then is the one who condemns? No one. Christ Jesus who died—more than that, who was raised to life—is at the right hand of God and is also interceding for us. ³⁵ Who shall separate us from the love of Christ? Shall trouble or hardship or persecution or famine or nakedness or danger or sword? ³⁶ As it is written: "For your sake we face death all day long; we are considered as sheep to be slaughtered." ³⁷ No, in all these things we are more than conquerors through him who loved us. ³⁸ For I am convinced that neither death nor life, neither angels nor demons, neither the present nor the future, nor any powers, ³⁹ neither height nor depth, nor anything else in all creation, will be able to separate us from the love of God that is in Christ Jesus our Lord. (Romans 8:31-39).

Look at this amazing list:
- No one can ultimately be against us (v. 31);
- God will give us "all things" as well as Jesus (v. 32);
- No one can condemn us: Christ died for us and now lives to pray for us (vv. 33-34);
- Nothing can separate us from Christ's love—nothing! (vv. 35-36);
- Instead, we can emerge as conquerors through all our trials (v. 37);
- Nothing in all of creation can separate us from God's love through Christ (vv. 38-39).

If we are to move from brokenness to wholeness it will only be possible as we look to Jesus, the "Wounded Healer," who Himself overcame not only pain and suffering but death itself all on our behalf. He has done everything necessary to enable us not to waste our pain, but to move beyond it to blessings not just for ourselves, but for many other broken ones who continue to suffer needlessly.

## Healer at Your Door

One of my favorite songs our daughter Rebecca has written is called, "Healer." I often had Rebecca sing this on *Nite Lite Live,* via videotape with her brother Joel. It became one of the most requested songs we ever played on the program because it spoke so powerfully to the hurting. The lyrics make the love of God not only apparent, but also meaningful to a world lost in suffering:

> Wounded come, there is salve for your sores
> Leave them open no more
> War-torn, find relief, here there is true peace
> Rest now complete, this house will never disappear
> There's a healer at your door, there's a healer at your door
> There's a healer at your door, healer at your door[14]

That Healer is Jesus.

# Further Reflection:

*"By His wounds we are healed"*
*(Isaiah 53:5)*

1. What do you say to yourself when someone wounds you? How could Paul's words in Romans 8:31-39 give you a new perspective on your situation?

2. Are you surprised that Jesus did not run away from pain in His life? How does that affect you?

3. Have you ever considered Jesus as your 'Wounded Healer' before?

4. Why does the cross give broken people hope, according to Isaiah 53:4-6; and Colossians 1:13-22?

5. Dr. Richard Dobbins stated, "It is what you say to the things that happen to you which is more important than the things that happen to you." Do you believe that to be true? If so, why?

## *"Jesus is our Wounded Healer!"*

Go to **www.DontWasteYourPain.com/book** or scan the code on the right for videos and other resources related to this chapter!

# Chapter 6: New Meaning for the Hurts of Life

"A life without pain could really hurt you," wrote the late missionary physician Dr. Paul Brand in *The Gift of Pain*, his memoir co-written with Philip Yancey.[15] Dr. Brand was a world renown surgeon who revolutionized treatment for those with leprosy and other skin diseases. A few years before he died, I had the privilege of arranging an interview with Dr. Brand on the television program, *100 Huntley Street*. Gloria and I were also blessed by being able to host him for two days while he was in town. In his book Dr. Brand tells about Tanya, a four-year-old patient he examined at the national leprosy hospital in Carville, Louisiana. Tanya's mother had brought her in for a diagnosis.

> A cloud of tension hung in the air between the little girl and her mother, but I noticed that Tanya seemed eerily unafraid. She sat on the edge of the padded table and watched impassively as I began to remove blood-soiled bandages from her feet. I thought it odd that she did not flinch or whimper as I removed the dressings next to her skin. She looked around the room with an expression of faint boredom. When I unwrapped the last bandage, I found grossly infected ulcers on the soles of both feet. Ever so gently I probed the wounds, glancing at Tanya's face for some reaction. She showed none.
>
> The probe pushed easily through soft, necrotic tissue, and I could even see the white gleam of bare

bone. Still no reaction from Tanya. Alas, I could offer little hope or comfort. I would do further tests, but it seemed apparent that Tanya suffered from a rare genetic defect known informally as "congenital indifference to pain." She was healthy in every respect but one: She did not feel pain. Nerves in her hands and feet transmitted messages about changes in pressure and temperature and so she felt a kind of tingling when she burned herself or hit a finger, but these carried no hint of unpleasantness. Tanya lacked any mental construct of pain. She rather enjoyed the tingling sensations, especially when they produced such dramatic reactions in others.

"We can get these wounds healed," I said, "but Tanya has no built-in warning system to defend her from further injury. Nothing will improve until Tanya understands the problem and consciously begins to improve herself."

Unfortunately, Tanya never did and by eleven was living a pathetic existence in an institution. She had lost both legs to amputation: she had refused to wear proper shoes and that, coupled with her failure to limp or to shift weight when standing (because she felt no discomfort), had eventually put intolerable pressure on her joints. Tanya had lost most of her fingers. Her elbows were constantly dislocated. She suffered the effects of chronic sepsis from ulcers on her hands and amputation stumps. Her tongue was lacerated and badly scarred from her nervous habit of chewing it. A monster, her father had called her. Tanya was no monster, only an extreme example of a human metaphor, really, of life without pain.[16]

Nobody really likes pain. We do our best to protect ourselves from it, run from it, medicate against it. And all that is normal. But what we often do not realize is, as Tanya's family found out, that physical pain can actually have a positive function in our lives: God has given it as an alert system in the body. As we learn what the pain means, and take positive steps in response, we can find a place of healing and strength. In this way pain is actually helpful for us. But if we choose to ignore or just numb the pain, moving forward as though nothing is wrong, we end up hurting ourselves even more. Not only so, but it hardens us to the pain that others feel as well.

We live in a culture that, like Tanya's body, has become desensitized to pain. In fact, Dr. Brand mentioned to me that the publisher had changed the title of the book from the original "Pain the Gift Nobody Wants" for the US market to *The Gift of Pain*, making the word *pain* less obvious in the title. This says something about North American society's aversion to the idea of pain. Dr. Brand concludes:

> "For good and for ill, the human species has among its privileges the preeminence of pain. We have the unique ability to step outside ourselves and self-reflect, by reading a book about pain, for example, or by summoning up the memory of a terrifying ordeal. Some pains—the pain of grief or emotional trauma—have no physical stimulus whatever. They are states of mind, concocted by the alchemy of the brain. These feats of consciousness make it possible for suffering to loiter in the mind long after the body's need for it has passed. Yet they also give us the potential to attain an outlook that will change the very landscape of the pain experience. *We can learn to cope, and even to triumph.*"[17]

## Joseph's Story

If there is one person in the Bible who learned not only to cope, but to triumph, through pain, it was Joseph. Ten times in thirteen chapters from Genesis 37-50 we are told that Joseph "wept," or "found a place to weep." With this ability to feel and to grieve, he went on to become one of the most compassionate and successful figures of his time, rescuing both his family and his nation from great suffering.

The Bible says that Joseph began his life as the favoured child of his father, Israel (Jacob). We are told that Israel, "loved Joseph more than any of his other sons" (Genesis 37:3). This made Joseph's older brothers jealous to the point that they could not even speak a kind word to him (Genesis 37:4). To make matters worse, Joseph told his family about a dream God had given him in which he rose to a position of authority over all of them. This, of course, only fueled his brothers' contempt for him. One day, Joseph's father sent him to check on his brothers, who were away tending the sheep. As he drew near, his brothers began plotting his demise. Intending to kill him, they grabbed him and threw him into a pit. Fortunately, Reuben, the eldest, pleaded for Joseph's life, and so instead of killing him, the brothers sold him into slavery to a passing caravan of Ishmaelites who were on their way to Egypt.

Once in Egypt, Joseph was bought by a wealthy man named Potiphar. Almost immediately Potiphar noticed Joseph's potential and put him in charge of the entire household. Things were looking up. Joseph was a handsome man; however, and he caught the eye of Potiphar's wife. Before long her not-so-subtle advances began: "Come to bed with me!" she demanded. Joseph declined. "No one is greater in this house than I am. My master has withheld nothing from me except you, because you are his wife. How then could I do such a wicked thing and sin against God?" (Genesis 39:9). One day when they were alone in the house, she grabbed Joseph's cloak demanding he sleep with her. Joseph fled, and as he did, she held onto his cloak, tearing it from him as he ran. When her husband returned, in her rage she lashed out against Joseph with a false accusation: "This Hebrew has been brought to us to make sport of us! He came in here to sleep with me, but I screamed. When he heard me scream for help he left his cloak beside me and ran out of the house" (Genesis 39:14-15). When Potiphar heard his wife's story, he "burned with anger" and sent Joseph to prison (Genesis 39:19-20).

It was a lot for one person to endure. Despised by his older brothers as a little boy and completely sold out by them in his early teens, Joseph would spend much of his young adulthood locked up in prison for a crime he did not commit. Yet instead of becoming bitter and vengeful, or giving up, he wept, forgave those who wronged him, and trusted that God would help him find a way out. This is suggested by the fact that the prison warden, "put Joseph in charge of all those held in the prison, and he was made responsible for all that was done there" (Genesis 39:22). Had Joseph been consumed by bitterness over his circumstances, it is hard to imagine the prison warden would have noticed his outstanding gifts of administration and been willing to entrust the running of the entire prison to an inmate (Genesis 39:23)!

God responded by giving Joseph a special ability to interpret dreams. Through a series of circumstances, Joseph interpreted a revelation from God given to Pharaoh. He was promoted to a high-level position as right-hand man to the king and ultimately, averted a national crisis in Egypt and saved his own family from starvation.

Joseph's decision to pour out his heart to God allowed the Lord to give him a new perspective on his situation, one that rid him of the emotional and psychological baggage that otherwise could have followed him the rest of his days. Eventually, Joseph came face to face with his brothers. With their fate now resting in Joseph's hands, he tested them to see whether they had changed their ways. When he saw that his brothers had indeed changed, Joseph compassionately used his position to help them out of their own season of suffering. He then spoke these redemptive words to his brothers: "You intended to harm me, but God intended it for good to accomplish what is now being done, the saving of many lives" (Genesis 50:20).

## When Your Dreams Go Up In Flames

One of the guests we had on *Nite Lite* was an amazing man named Mickey Robinson. Mickey had grown up in a rough family and turned to thrill-seeking to escape his abject home life. What he loved more than anything was the rush from sky-diving!

Once, at just nineteen years of age, he went up on a routine skydive, but to everyone's horror, in the middle of the plane's ascent, the engine suddenly failed! Out of control, the plane plummeted toward the ground, hit some trees, cartwheeled, then burst into flames. The pilot was burned alive, but somehow Mickey survived – but barely. He had third-degree burns from head to foot, his right eye was burned and blinded, his feet burned and almost useless because of extensive nerve damage. He could not eat on his own but had to be fed through a tube; thus going from a muscular 170 pounds down to just 90 pounds. Although the medical team tried to save Mickey, he slipped into a coma and the doctors eventually gave up all hope for his survival. After conferring with one another, the doctors called the family to come and say their final goodbyes.

That day, teetering between life and death, Mickey had an out-of-body experience, more real than anything he had ever felt before. He sensed smothering darkness and with a look of horror caught a glimpse of a bottomless pit that he was moving towards. In that moment he began to cry out, "God, give me another chance!" Instantly as he cried out he felt God's presence and suddenly found himself back in the hospital room, alert – and speaking in another language! Peace filled his heart, washing over him, drowning out the pain and fear. From that day on he knew God was at work in his life. To the shock of his doctors and family, he came out of the coma and began to improve: his sight slowly returned, and the nerves in his legs were miraculously restored.

In more ways than one Mickey walked out of that hospital a different man than he went in. But although he had found hope in God, that did not mean the end of his pain. It would take 50 surgeries and years of rehabilitation to get back to some sense of normalcy. Even then, his face was severely disfigured and people would just stare at him in the street. Some days this would be overwhelming and Mickey would think, *could anyone ever love me*? Yet he never forgot his experience with God or the supernatural power that had flooded his life.

Eventually, Mickey was connected with a church, discipled in the faith, and grew deeper in the Lord. Along the way he met and married his wife, Barbara and they travel the world testifying of God's grace in the midst of pain and tragedy.

On *Nite Lite* he shared, "I've seen many miracles, but the greatest miracle is being born again, and experiencing the love of God!" Today Mickey is involved in a worldwide ministry where he brings hope to the hopeless and the reality of a personal relationship with Jesus Christ that changes not only how we see life, but how we do life.

> **Our success in life depends not on how well we can protect ourselves from painful experiences, but on how well we respond to them.**

You can read more about his amazing story in his book "Falling into Heaven."[18]

Mickey's story, and the story of Joseph in Scripture, teach us that our success in life depends not on how well we can protect ourselves from painful experiences, but on how well we respond to them.

Mickey could have given up in despair or discouragement, overwhelmed by pain, rejection, and shattered dreams. Yet he did not give up! He allowed God to use him, not just 'in spite of' his pain, but because of the pain he had gone through!

Joseph responded to his suffering not by continuing to complain about how unjust it was, but by praying, forgiving, and waiting for God to give him the wisdom and the opportunity he needed to get out of his painful circumstances and move on with his life. But not only was Joseph able to move on, the things he learned in the season of hurt and rejection actually enabled him to lead and be used of God in greater ways. In the next chapter, we will see how painful experiences can actually equip us to make a difference in our broken world.

### Life Is Hard, but God is Good

*You turn the key*
*Then close the door behind you*
*Drop your bags on the floor*
*You reach for the light*
*But there's darkness deep inside*
*And you can't take it anymore*

*'Cause sometimes living takes the life out of you*
*And sometimes living is all you can do*

*Life is hard, the world is cold*
*We're barely young and then we're old*
*But every falling tear is always understood*
*Yes, life is hard, but God is good*

*You start to cry*
*'Cause you've been strong for so long*
*And that's not how you feel*
*You try to pray*
*But there's nothing left to say*
*So you just quietly kneel*

*In the silence of all that you face*
*God will give you His mercy and grace*
*Jesus never said*
*It was an easy road to travel*
*He only said that you would never be alone*
*So when your last thread of hope*
*Begins to come unraveled*
*Don't give up, He walks beside you*
*On this journey home and He knows*

*Life is hard, the world is cold*
*We're barely young and then we're old*
*But every falling tear is always understood*
*Yes, life is hard, but God is good*

—Pam Thum[19]

# FURTHER REFLECTION:

*"You intended to harm me, but God intended it for good to accomplish what is now being done, the saving of many lives."*
*(Genesis 50:20)*

1. Dr. Paul Brand suggests that a life without pain can really hurt you. How have the hurts in your life helped you?

2. Where did Mickey Robinson get the courage to keep going?

3. Can you identity with the story of Joseph? What does his story say to you about God's purpose for your life? (See Genesis 50:18-20; as well as Psalm 34:15-19; Jeremiah 15:10; Philippians 2:12, 13).

4. How have you responded to the people that caused you pain? Would you like to respond differently? If so, how?

*"God can give new meaning to the pain of our past!"*

Go to **www.DontWasteYourPain.com/book** or scan the code on the right for videos and other resources related to this chapter!

# Chapter 7: Equipped Through Brokenness

### Alive Now!

In the months that followed I shared my vision with our church board of deacons and asked only for their blessing, not for any financial assistance. Gloria and I were making only $90 a week at the time, but we went out on a limb and borrowed $3,000 from the bank. The two-night pilot aired on CKWS TV in Kingston, Ontario, from 11:45 p.m. to 1:00 a.m. Cam Shillington, a friend I had known for quite a few years, worked at CKWS. He had a nationally syndicated program called *Gospel Singin' Time*, with his own gospel group, "The Masters." A year before, Cam had helped me to start a radio program called *Reachout* on CKWS-FM. It aired every Sunday morning at 9:30 a.m. and was a thirty-minute mixture of gospel music and encouragement from the Bible. Now that the Lord was putting this new burden on my heart, I naturally turned to Cam for advice and direction about helping me to produce *Alive Now!*

Gloria and I took out the bank loan and booked the CKWS-TV studio and crew to shoot the pilot for *Alive Now!* Cam suggested we ask Lorne Shepherd, one of the directors at CKWS-TV and a strong follower of Jesus, to direct *Alive Now!* Lorne's many years of experience and his understanding of the purpose of our program was key to its success. Another important aspect of the pilot was setting up four telephones in the studio so that those watching *Alive Now!* could phone in and pray with one of the four pastors taking the calls. They included my good friend Pastor Jack Richards, who oversaw the call-in part of the program, along with Pastors Bob Masters, Meg Lewis, and Keith Gonyou.

With a talented television crew assembled and a pastoral presence on the telephone lines, I now began the process of putting together the program's content. What would it look like? Who should I have on the program?

Through prayer, I eventually decided to focus on well-known Canadian believers. Because of my love for sports, it seemed the Lord was encouraging me to invite Christian athletes from baseball, football, and the Canadian Olympic Team. I wrote Cy Young Award winner Ferguson "Fergie" Jenkins of the Boston Red Sox, whom I had recently met while visiting Lance Peterson, a college friend in Boston. I also wrote Peter Mueller of the Toronto Argonauts, Gary Lefebvre and Ron Estay of the Edmonton Eskimos, Wayne Tosh and Rod Woodward of the Ottawa Rough Riders, and Hugh Fraser of the Canadian Olympic Track and Field Team. I shared the vision for the show with each of them. Two other important people I invited were David Mainse who was the host of *Crossroads*, a weekly half-hour television program that aired across Canada on Sundays, and Keith Parks, a district youth director who was a strong spiritual influence in my life. Each of these individuals responded in the positive. *Alive Now!* was really going to happen!

As the day of the first live broadcast drew near, Cam helped me make a rundown for the two programs. Much prayer went into the preparation of this live pilot since there was no opportunity for a dress rehearsal. Though we did include a couple of "canned" songs by the Imperials and Henry and Hazel Slaughter, everything else was live—the guests, the studio audience, and the music (The Masters). They were all live—incredible! To our knowledge, no other late-night Christian television phone-in program had ever before been broadcast live in Canada.

As I drove to the studio on the big day, I was aware that the success of this venture depended totally upon the Lord. This was brand new territory for me. If the Lord did not help, I would be in big trouble! However, He did help us. From the moment Lorne Shepherd gave the ten-second countdown and I opened with,

"Welcome to *Alive Now!*" a marked sense of the presence and power of God was evident. To all who phoned or wrote in, we offered a free book, *The Freedom of Forgiveness* by David Augsburger.

As soon as the telephone number was put up on the screen, the phones began to light up with people calling in from all over the televised area to share their many needs with our telephone pastors. The pastors prayed with them for healing, resolving marriage issues, family restoration, and salvation. As people called in we showed footage from the Canadian Football League and interviewed the players we had invited. They each shared how they had come to know Jesus Christ as their personal Savior and Lord, then Wayne Tosh walked over to the prayer lines and took a live call from a viewer! This segment was followed by Hugh Fraser of the Olympic Track and Field Team. We closed the show with youth director Keith Parks' animated and lively sharing of the gospel! Before we knew it, the first night was over. How had the time gone by so quickly? Those of us who were part of that first program agreed that the Lord had been present as lives had been touched and changed. Yes, the first pilot of *Alive Now!* was a success!

The following night captured a lot of interest as I interviewed sports icon Fergie Jenkins. He talked about his faith and the spiritual influence his mother had had on him. Next, David Mainse of *Crossroads* came on and shared from his heart, encouraging people to believe that God would meet them where they were. He was really energized by the live studio audience and by the phone lines, which provided instant two-way communication with the viewer—not to mention by the incredible sense of God's presence. After the program was over, David said, "Paul, what you've done tonight is what I want to do every day across Canada. Can we talk?"

In a meeting two weeks later, David shared his vision for daily Christian television across Canada and asked me to join him in this venture. We met again a few weeks later as David wanted to show me a possible location he had found to begin this new ministry. We drove to 100 Huntley Street in Toronto, which was owned in those days by Confederation Life Insurance. David liked the number 100 in the street address; he said it represented the 100 percent living that knowing Jesus allows. Because he did not want the name to have a religious or churchy sound to it, he was considering calling this new program *100 Huntley Street*. At the end of that day, I confirmed that I would work with David as an associate producer. His wife, Norma Jean, would be the producer. I would discover her to be a woman with an incredible love for God, for people, and one of the most compassionate leaders I had ever met. It would be a privilege to help her research and find guests for this new program.

I left the meeting feeling overwhelmed that this well-known television preacher would ask a young pastor from a small Ontario town to join him in this new venture of faith. There was much to think and pray about. As I shared with Gloria and we prayed together, we both became certain that this opportunity was from the Lord.

Looking back I am again reminded that God can use us, despite the painful circumstances we have gone through. In fact, He often uses us *because of the pain* we have gone through. It gives us the empathy needed to minister to others who are hurting. It also gives us the grace to move forward with humility.

## Equipped Through The School Of Pain

The good thing about brokenness is that it shows us we were never meant to live our lives apart from God. In fact, our brokenness equips us with the compassion needed to care for others, as the Scriptures state:

> Praise be to the God and Father of our Lord Jesus Christ, the Father of compassion and the God of all comfort, who comforts us in all our troubles, *so that we can comfort those in any trouble with the comfort we*

> *ourselves receive from God.* For just as we share abundantly in the sufferings of Christ, so also our comfort abounds through Christ. If we are distressed, it is for your comfort and salvation; if we are comforted, it is for your comfort, which produces in you patient endurance of the same sufferings we suffer. (2 Corinthians 1:3-6; emphasis mine).

In a very real way, our brokenness can become our greatest source of strength as we learn to trust in the Lord for His provision. Jesus is our Redeemer; so we should not be surprised that our brokenness can be redeemed and become our greatest source of strength as we learn to give it to Him.

Regarding God's comfort, Dr. Ajith Fernando states,

> By opening ourselves to God's comfort we also open ourselves to healing from bitterness. We are bitter when we think of an event in purely negative terms. If God has comforted us, even though the memory of the event is still painful, the bitterness will be gone because we have experienced a love that is greater than the harm done to us. Having experienced God's comfort we are also able to face people, even people who have hurt us, with God's grace, which is greater than all sin. So we can be a constructive presence in unpleasant and angry situations. Our bitterness is gone. Now our full energies are given to finding a resolution rather than showing that we are right or teaching the person who hurt us a lesson.[20]

Isn't it amazing what God's grace can do in our lives? Later in that same letter to the Corinthians Paul shared how his own experience of pain and weakness enabled him to show God's power more clearly: "My grace is sufficient for you, for my power is made perfect in weakness," God had told him. So Paul could say, "That is why, for Christ's sake, I delight in weaknesses, in insults, in hardships, in persecutions, in difficulties. For when I am weak, then I am strong" (2 Corinthians 12:9,10).

Not only do we gain compassion from our pain; it also enables us to point back to God and display His power in a special way. It is like a billboard that shouts: "There's no way I could do this on my own!" Like Gideon's army, our weakness can reveal God's power and be the channel for His healing to come to others as well.

### Gideon, The Reluctant Hero

The Bible says that Gideon was just a young man when an angel appeared and shocked him with the news that God had chosen him to lead the people of Israel. This was during a very difficult time in Israel's history. Israel had been so severely oppressed by the Midianites, that they were living in constant fear, even hiding in caves so they could not be found. Anything they planted was stolen, all

> **Our brokenness equips us with the compassion needed to care for others**

their livestock was likewise taken or killed. They were so impoverished, poor, and fearful that they finally cried out to God in the midst of their pain. But then the angel appeared to Gideon, telling him "God is with you!" Gideon was taken aback, stunned that God would call him of all people for this job. Gideon had a lot of questions – and a lot of excuses! They may sound familiar to you:

"If God is with us, why did this happen to us?" he asked (see Judges 7:13). Like many of us, he probably thought God was not interested in his life or did not care about his people anymore. Things had gotten so bad that the Israelites probably felt that God had abandoned them. Or maybe they began to doubt the stories they had heard – maybe it was all made up and God did not exist anyway!

But even standing face-to-face with an angel Gideon still doubted. "How can God use me? My family is nothing, and I am the least in my family, I'm good-for-nothing!" (Judges 7:15 – my paraphrase!) I do not know if you have ever felt that way, but I sure have. With all my doubts, fears, hurts, and brokenness, I've wondered, "How can God ever use me? Sure, He can use someone stronger or smarter, or the person who seems like they have everything all together, but me? No way!" Yet the Lord is gracious. He did not give up on Gideon, and He will not give up on you, either! In Gideon's case, the Lord even spoke a further word of encouragement to him: "I will be with you" (verse 16).

The rest of Gideon's story details how he set out with 32,000 men to attack the Midianites. Even with all those fighters, Gideon was still fearful. Yet God told him something strange: "you've got too many men, Gideon! If you win with all your troops you'll boast about your own strength!" So God instructed Gideon to send a bunch of soldiers home. He eventually ended up with a handful of men (300) against an army of trained and fierce fighters. But God worked miraculously and Israel defeated the whole Midianite army. And guess what? It was God – not Gideon or his army – who got the glory!

Gideon's story illustrates what the apostle Paul was talking about when he said that it is during those times when we are weak that God can show Himself strong. When we do not hide our brokenness, but offer it to God, He can use it and make something beautiful, something victorious, out of our life!

### Hope to Millions

One of the people that really exemplifies this principle is Joni Eareckson-Tada. When I eventually became the Guest Coordinator of 100 Huntley Street in 1977, Joni was one of our first guests on the program. Ten years earlier, when she was just 16, Joni had broken her neck in a diving accident and become a quadriplegic.

It was a devastating experience for Joni. All her friends were graduating and heading off to college, but she was stuck in a hospital with no hope of ever walking or using her arms again. Depression set in and she began to doubt God and question why He would let this happen. She never did regain control of her limbs, spending the rest of her life in a wheelchair, unable to do even the most basic tasks such as dress herself. But as the years went by she began to recognize God's hand was still on her life. She began to paint (using a brush she held in her mouth) and then sell her paintings, which were in high demand...eventually landing her a spot on the Today Show" in 1974, and relative fame.

In 1976 (the year before she came on the show), she released her autobiography: *Joni: The unforgettable story of a young woman's struggle against quadriplegia & depression*. It quickly became an international best-seller, highlighting how her faith gave meaning and hope despite her pain and disabilities.

Her story was an inspiration to millions and I was able to arrange for her to join us on the program where she shared from her heart about her trust and dependence on the Lord through a life of pain. That evening my wife Gloria and I had the privilege to take Joni to the CN Tower Restaurant high above Toronto where we enjoyed a delicious dinner and time of sharing together. There we heard more of Joni's story, her love for the Lord, and His ability to bring purpose from her pain. It was so encouraging to see how she was able to grow closer to God through her hurt and hardship. Now more than 50 years since that accident, Joni continues to tell the story and the reality that the Lord Jesus did not waste her pain. In fact, because of all that she has been through, Joni's life continues to be an inspiration around the world. She has authored 40 books, has a daily radio program, recorded many songs, been in films and received multiple awards for her work in helping those with disabilities. Her pain equipped her to minister God's healing in a special way to those with similar disabilities, and allowed her to bring hope and life to those in despair!

Not all of us will have the same platform that Joni has had. But all of us have opportunities to serve others and to minister God's healing to those around us. Like the apostle Paul had stated, and as Joni learned, our own sufferings can equip us to be channels of God's compassion and care to those that are in need.

# Further Reflection

*"Praise be to the God and Father of our Lord Jesus Christ,
the Father of compassion and the God of all comfort,
who comforts us in all our troubles, so that we can comfort those
in any trouble with the comfort we ourselves receive from God."*
*(2 Corinthians 1:3-4)*

1. Do you believe that our brokenness can become our greatest source of strength?

2. How is God's grace shown through our weakness?

3. Like Gideon, have you ever felt that God could not use you?

4. If you were Joni Eareckson, how do you think you would have responded?

5. Have you ever considered that the 'school of pain' is essential if we are ever going to help others?

*"Our pain equips us to minister healing to others!"*

Go to **www.DontWasteYourPain.com/book** or scan the code on the right for videos and other resources related to this chapter!

# Chapter 8: God Can Turn Your Life Around!

In February 1977, we bade farewell to our special congregation at Tweed Pentecostal Church. They had graciously welcomed us into their hearts and homes over the previous three years, and they were an integral part of the healing process for me. Gloria and I packed our things in a small U-Haul truck with the help of my brothers and made our way to Toronto. Gloria's parents kindly invited us to live with them until we could find a place of our own. It would be two months before I received my first paycheck, but that did not matter because we were so excited about how God was fulfilling the vision He had given me. Once David Mainse signed the lease for the building on Huntley Street many devoted individuals went to work turning the former recreation center into a television studio and ministry centre. I can still remember those early days before we went to air, getting the office furniture in and setting up shop with Valerie James, David's Executive Assistant, Father Bob MacDougall, and Pastor Clyde Williamson, the two men whom David had hired before me, and Ann (Gamble) Hilsden, the music coordinator. The excitement was growing!

June 15, 1977, quickly arrived, and to the excitement of thousands, *100 Huntley Street* went to air live across Canada on the Global Television Network. It was an incredible day and an awesome privilege to be there as part of that historic moment. Since then it has become the longest-running daily television show in Canada's history! One of the unique aspects of the program was its interdenominational flavor. Father Bob MacDougall was a Roman Catholic priest; Reverend Al Reimers an Anglican priest; Reverend Jim Poynter, a Free Methodist minister; and Reverends Don Osborne, Clyde Williamson, and I were Pentecostal ministers.

Later, United Church minister Reverend Gord Williams joined the staff.

Viewers could call into the live phones in the studio and be prayed for to receive Jesus Christ as Saviour, or as Healer of a broken body, or a broken heart. The presence of God was tangible in the studio. There was also a studio audience to care for and minister to, as well as busloads of people who came to be part of the live program every morning. Generally, they did not leave until after lunch and a special time of prayer. Off the air, David was always working hard—and every staff member followed his lead—to get ready for the next program.

That summer I was asked to co-host *100 Huntley Street* with David for a week. I was only twenty-six years old! I felt deeply honored that David, a man with seemingly infinite energy and creative ideas, was willing to take a risk on a much younger man. As the time drew near for the first program I would co-host with David, I began to feel nervous about what to say.

Two things made a difference for me. One was the wisdom of Proverbs 16:1 (KJV): "The preparation of the heart belongs to man, but the answer of the tongue is from the Lord." My part was to prepare my heart in prayer; God's part was to speak through me when I opened my mouth! This may sound oversimplified, but it really spoke to my heart and laid a foundation for prayer in preparation for every program. Oswald Chambers in his devotional book, *My Utmost for His Highest* said it like this, "Prayer does not equip us for greater works—prayer is the greater work."[21] David led the way in this regard; he vowed to spend as much time on his knees in prayer *before the program* as he did on the air *during the program*. The program ran for ninety minutes, so David arrived around 4:30 or 5:00 a.m., while it was still dark, to make sure he had time for private prayer with the Lord. Then, thirty minutes before going to air, the on-air team would meet in the green room for prayer led by David on his knees, or sometimes on his face, but always humbled before the Lord in intercessory prayer. How grateful I was for that example!

Help also came from Father Bob McDougall, a key part of the ministry of *100 Huntley Street*. When I shared with Father Bob what I was feeling, he wisely said, "Paul, if you're ever about to go on air and you're *not* nervous, don't go on! You'll blow it!" Those two pieces of advice helped me realize my dependence on God and that this ministry was not about me. Rather, it was about God sharing His heart and His message through me to the people Jesus had died for. God knew who would be watching.

During these early years I helped arrange for hundreds of people to appear on the program. It was amazing to hear their stories and see how God could take the difficulties of life and turn them around for His glory and the good of others! There are far too many to recount all their stories here, but there are a few that stand out in my memory.

## Billy Graham

In 1978 Billy Graham had a crusade in Toronto. He was on 100 Huntley Street and was interviewed by David Mainse.[22] One of the encouraging words Billy shared was that Canada could help lead the world in a spiritual awakening – in part because of Canada's stand for peace and the respect Canada had on the global stage. I had the privilege of arranging for Billy to meet with the media in Toronto. It was amazing to see the respect they gave him – even though most were not believers. I will always remember Mr. Graham's humility and the real sense that we were in the presence of a man of God.

## Life in Prison to Life in Jesus!

Ernie Hollands had spent 25 years in a Maximum Security Penitentiary for bank robbery and shooting at a police officer. He had somehow managed to escape 5 times, but was recaptured each time and locked away for good. The Parole Board had told him he would never be paroled because he was incorrigible and a danger to society. Ernie seemingly had lived a totally wasted life – a life of sin, cheating, and godlessness.

During his years in prison, he learned to tie fish flies to pass the time (he had lots of time!) and eventually became so good at it that he would sell them to sporting goods stores.

One store Ernie sent a sample to was "Bailey's Sports Center Ltd" in Pembroke, Ontario, owned by Grant Bailey who was a strong believer. Grant wrote a reply letter informing Ernie that he liked the fish flies and would sell them in his store. But Mr. Bailey also shared with Ernie in his letter how he had been empty and his life void of meaning until he had opened his heart and life to Jesus Christ through prayer. Soon Grant and his family came to visit Ernie and brought him a Bible along with Christian magazines. These prison visits continued every month for 18 months. The Lord began to work in Ernie's heart and on March 12, 1975, at 2:00 a.m. Jesus appeared to Ernie, told him he was giving him a new chance in life and Ernie was dramatically changed!

The next morning, in front of all the rough characters in the penitentiary, Ernie carried his Bible out in the prison yard shouting praises to Jesus. Well, they thought he had lost his mind! He had not lost it, but rather had his mind renewed by the power of Jesus!

Another miracle was soon to come for Ernie – just over a year later, in April 1976, he was released from prison for good – a free man! No one could explain how that happened, but he walked out a free man – both inside and out!

After that, for many years Ernie travelled across North America and around the globe telling the story of God's amazing grace in forgiving and changing a man like him. Years later Gloria and I were privileged to reconnect with Ernie and have him in our home, recounting the amazing ways that God had worked in his life. If God can take someone like Ernie and change his life around, he can do that for anyone!

Ernie eventually wrote a book about his life titled, "Hooked" with Doug Brendel. Thousands of copies of his book have been sent to prisoners all over the world free and postage paid.

During this time, Ernie spoke in hundreds of churches and on major television programs before his death in 1996. His widow Sheila continues his work through Hebron Ministries, which they began in 1992.

## Brother Andrew

We had Brother Andrew on the program in 1978, ten years after his book "God's Smuggler" was released. Born into a poor family, with parents who struggled with health, he grew into a rebellious youth, longing for adventure and for some way to escape small-town life.

When he was eleven World War II broke out, turning his relatively routine life upside-down. His teenage years were spent trying to cause as much trouble for the occupiers as possible and he eventually joined the Dutch Resistance Army against the Nazis, fighting for freedom for his homeland.

After the war, when he was 18 he went as a soldier to Indonesia (the Dutch East Indies at the time) where he witnessed terrible atrocities on a regular basis. Deeply troubled by what he saw Andrew turned to alcohol to numb himself from the horrors around him. Once during the fighting, he was severely injured when he was hit in the ankle with a bullet and nearly had his leg amputated. During his time in rehabilitation, the faith of some of the nurses reawakened his curiosity about the things of God. He began to read the Bible and go back to church, where he finally surrendered his life to the Lord.

God eventually used his adventurous spirit as Andrew went deep into communist territory, secretly meeting with believers and smuggling Bibles to them. His book "God's Smuggler" which tells of the many adventures he had behind the 'iron curtain' has sold over 15 million copies and inspired believers around the world.

Brother Andrew was a joy to be around, his faith was vibrant and infectious! After the program we went back to the hotel where we both were staying and had a memorable dinner together as he shared more of his story. It was a fairly nice hotel that, for promotion and advertising reasons, let *100 Huntley Street* guests stay there for free. Later that evening he called to my room phone, and with much laughter and disbelief said, "Paul, you'll never believe it, they have a gold plated phone in the bathroom!"

Brother Andrew could have given up – alone in a hospital, facing the possibility of amputation, his country threatened by war, his young life already scarred by seeing too much bloodshed. But when he reached out to God, he found hope and healing! God turned his life around and used it in a mighty way to give hope to others, and to bring God's word to places where it was illegal to have the Bible. Like Andrew, we never know the amazing things God might do when we surrender our lives to Him!

## Keith Green

Another person we had the privilege of having on 100 Huntley Street during those early days was Keith Green. (Ann Hilsden, who was the music coordinator at the time, arranged for him to be on the show). I will always remember him sitting down at the piano with his big mop of hair and banging out his amazing songs on the piano. Such passion and energy and love for the Lord!

Fast forward a few years when we got the news, in May 1982, that Keith had been in a tragic plane crash that took his life as well as the lives of two of his small children and some friends of the family. We were shocked by such a heart-breaking and seemingly senseless loss of life. When this tragic accident happened, one of the things that helped sustain Melody Green, Keith's widow, was the verse from John 12:24, "unless a kernel of wheat falls to the ground and dies, it remains only a single seed. But if it dies, it produces many seeds."[23] Indeed, as she came to see, millions of lives were touched and impacted not only through Keith's life, but also through his death and the testimony of his passion for God during his brief time on earth.

## Fruit from Darkness

God has given us many wonderful parallels in nature that help us understand spiritual realities. Often in the Scriptures we see Jesus using everyday objects to illustrate great truth. One of Jesus' favourites was to talk about farm life – something very familiar to His hearers. He spoke of a farmer sowing seeds, or of a vineyard that needed tending. One time, in speaking of His death Jesus said those words about a kernel of wheat dying, being buried, so it can produce a harvest of many seeds.

For a plant to grow, a seed needs to be buried in the soil. It is a picture of death and pain, of darkness and loneliness. Unless it is planted it will not bear fruit.

Many times in our lives we also feel like that seed – buried, forgotten, alone. But, like the seed, if we allow God's presence to fill our lives He can cause us to grow and to be fruitful. It's not easy. And it may take some time. There may be further pruning involved. But as the great Gardener of our lives, we can trust Him to know what He is doing and to bring us to a place of fruitfulness!

## Naomi's Pain: From Bitter to Blessed

One of the many examples of this in Scripture is seen in the life of Naomi. I imagine that she must have spent many nights weeping, crying out to God, wondering why her dreams had been shattered and buried.

Naomi and her husband Elimelech, along with their two sons, Mahlon and Kilion, left Israel due to a severe famine. They headed as refugees for Moab, a country neighbouring Israel. Not long after, Elimelech tragically died. Naomi was devastated yet grateful that she still had her two sons with her. She soon found wives for them: Mahlon married Orpah and Kilion married Ruth. As hard as it was to imagine tragedy struck Naomi again within ten years of her husband's death: her two sons died.

Naomi could not bear the pain. She viewed her losses the way many people do and concluded that God was against her. Perhaps

Naomi wondered, "Aren't I part of God's people? Doesn't God see me or care for me anymore?" Resentment began to seep into Naomi's soul. We can sense it in her words: "It is more bitter for me than for you, because the Lord's hand has turned against me!" (Ruth 1:13). In fact, Naomi told her friends to call her "Mara" instead of Naomi, because Mara meant "bitter." She was beginning to form her identity around her circumstances, rather than on what God thought of her, or had planned for her. Because of her pain Naomi thought her story was finished; she was unable to see how God could bring anything good out of something that appeared to be so bad.

We all need to be careful about how we interpret the bad things that happen to us. In deep sorrow Naomi gave up and advised her two daughters-in-law to go back home and find new husbands. Orpah followed her suggestion, but Ruth refused. "Don't urge me to leave you or to turn back from you," Ruth replied. "Where you go I will go, and where you stay I will stay. Your people will be my people and your God my God. Where you die I will die, and there I will be buried. May the Lord deal with me, be it ever so severely, if even death separates you and me" (Ruth 1:16). Could there be any stronger example of devotion in all of Scripture? Ruth's willingness to selflessly bind herself to one in such tragedy and suffering is amazing. However, in the throes of depression, Naomi was unable to see her world correctly.

> **We need to be careful how we interpret the bad things that happen to us.**

A small glimmer of hope for Naomi emerged in her daughter-in-law's promises to never leave her, never forsake her. It is the same promise that God makes to us: "Never will I leave you; never will I forsake you" (Hebrews 13:5-6). We begin to see how, in a sense, Ruth is like God and sometimes we are like Naomi; though many will leave us and forsake us, God will not.

Ruth's promise did not take away Naomi's pain, but it did help her begin to move in the right direction and kept her going until she reached a place where she could say, "God is good."

If you read through the story, in the book of Ruth, you will see how after Naomi and Ruth returned to Israel, God moved the heart of Boaz to provide for Ruth and then to eventually marry her. They had a child, Obed, who would eventually become the grandfather of David, the great King of Israel. Hundreds of years later, of course, Jesus himself would come from David's lineage.

But let's think about Naomi once again. Imagine her in Moab, her husband and two sons suddenly gone. All her dreams suddenly shattered, her longings unfulfilled, her hopes dashed to pieces. She put a label on herself: "bitter." But looking back we

> **God is able to turn bitterness into blessing.**

see that God actually had blessing in store for her. What if she had really given up? Turned her back on God? She could have said, "I never want to go back to Israel and its God! He doesn't care about me!" But, no, even though she could not understand it, she returned again. And as we turn to the Lord, even in the midst of pain, God can turn our bitterness to blessing, just as he did for Naomi! When our circumstances look desperate and we are tempted to become despondent, we must remember that there is still hope.

So, don't give up. God is near. Turn your eyes toward heaven and know that He sees your tears. Let Him draw you close to Himself. Rest there in His embrace and allow Him to "quiet you with his love" (Zephaniah 3:17). Yes, loss is a bitter pill to take, but we never know what good God will bring out of it, or the greater plan He can unfold if we only trust Him.

### Gaining Understanding

I had been working with David Mainse for about a year and a half. One morning after the program, a well-dressed young man came into the foyer of the building. As soon as I introduced myself and greeted him, I had a sudden sense in my heart, "This man will take your job."

I learned that his name was Dan Statham and he had a cable program in the Oshawa area. Within a week a telephone call came from Pastor Glen Pitts, who had become the new senior pastor at Kingston Gospel Temple in Kingston, Ontario. He asked if I would join him as his associate pastor. When I shared this with David, he said, "Paul, I don't want you to go. If you want, you can begin the late-night program like *Alive Now!* that you did in Kingston, but please don't leave." We had previously talked about my hosting a new show like *Alive Now,* but I knew inside that I was not yet ready to host the late-night program. Though I could not articulate it at that time, I had an inner awareness that I simply had not suffered enough. What could I possibly say at age twenty-seven to people who were going through difficult and traumatic times? How was I to understand their pain when I had known relatively little myself? And so, with many tears, I said good-bye to David and Norma Jean and our *100 Huntley Street* family. Though I did not know it at the time, twenty years would pass before David and I would work together in ministry again on *100 Huntley Street* and the late-night program he went on to create, *Nite Lite Live.*

Gloria and I had a tremendous time in Kingston with Glen and Jeanette Pitts. Glen was a real mentor to me and I have never forgotten Glen's valuable imprint on my life.

Sometime later an invitation came from Queensway Cathedral in Toronto for me to serve as the youth and young adult pastor to a congregation of over 3,000 people. It was a time of tremendous spiritual awakening in the church with many coming to know the Lord. As well as leading the youth I also had the opportunity to help with counseling and hospital visitation which taught me much about empathizing with people in the painful seasons of their lives.

I was still learning about brokenness and discovering how to minister God's love to those going through pain. What I did not know was that soon Gloria and I were going to witness brokenness on a scale we had never known before.

# Further Reflection

*"The Lord mocks the mockers, but is gracious to the humble."*
(Proverbs 3:34, NLT)

1. A seed needs to be buried before it can bring forth fruit. Have you ever felt 'buried' before? Do you believe God can bring fruit out of your life and experiences?

2. How did God use Brother Andrew's experiences of pain to fulfil His purpose for his life?

3. Naomi called herself "bitter," feeling that God had forsaken her and given her a bitter life and future. Have you ever felt that way before?

4. No doubt Ruth was devastated by the loss of her husband. What can you learn from her response to this loss that will help you turn your pain into gain?

*"God can bring fruitfulness out of difficult experiences!"*

Go to **www.DontWasteYourPain.com/book** or scan the code on the right for videos and other resources related to this chapter!

# Chapter 9: The Pain of Loss and Shattered Dreams

Our time at Queensway Cathedral became a real season of growth for Gloria and I, both in ministry and as parents. Then in the early 1980s as the church entered into a season of tremendous spiritual awakening, the Lord began to speak to myself and Gloria about a new adventure for our family – overseas missions.

It all began in July of 1981 when Gloria shared with me that, as a young girl of eight years of age, she had felt the Lord put a burden on her heart for missionary work in Africa. As we talked and prayed about this, the Lord began to lay a burden for missionary work on my heart as well.

As a teenager when I gave my heart to the Lord, He immediately gave me a passion for evangelism; a desire to help people to know Jesus as Savior and Lord. However, I had never translated that passion into missionary work; I had always focused on Canada. But now here we were as a young married couple with three children talking about going overseas to minister cross-culturally. The more we talked and prayed, the more excited we became. We felt the next step was to contact the Missions Department of the denomination with whom I held my ordination credentials. The Director informed us of three countries in Africa that needed immediate help: Liberia, Uganda, and Malawi. I asked which of those countries seemed to have the greatest need, to which he answered, "Uganda." "Then that is where we want to go," we responded. The Director then shared with us that they had already asked a senior missionary couple if they would be willing to transition to Uganda. If they said 'yes' we would need to consider one of the other two countries. If they declined the invitation, then we would be able to go to Uganda.

We left that meeting full of excitement now that we were on the path of fulfilling Gloria's dream. Most of the family and close friends we shared our news with were encouraging. Some though, were not: "Oh Paul, please don't take your wife and three precious children to Uganda!" I began to get cold feet and thought, *Is this really God, or is it just our idea?*

A few days later, on a Tuesday morning, I felt that I had to get an answer to that question. As a result, I left my office at Queensway Cathedral and went into the small chapel, got down on my knees by one of the chairs, and cried out, "Jesus, what do You want us to do? Is this idea of going to Uganda just our wild imagination, or is this You?" Immediately, I sensed the Holy Spirit speaking to my heart: "Hebrews 4:6." Because I did not know this text offhand, I turned to the Scripture, and there in my Bible (the King James Version at the time), I read, "Seeing it remaineth that some must enter therein, and they to whom it was first preached entered not in because of unbelief." Immediately, I knew the other couple was going to say "no" to Uganda. Peace overwhelmed my spirit and I realized we were on track; we had no need to be afraid. And that is exactly what happened. As we finished our time at Queensway Cathedral, the pastor and church board graciously announced that they would support us entirely during our first four-year term in Uganda – an incredible blessing. We were sent out by our wonderful church family with their prayers and their support.

Our final weeks in Canada were taken up with packing and getting our crate ready to be shipped to Africa. Finally, the day arrived, a day that is forever etched in my mind. We gathered our three children, all under the age of 6 together, and there in the airport terminal surrounded by our families, my dad prayed for protection, favour, and blessing of the Lord to be upon us.

Over the years I had been learning about pain – the pain of abuse, the pain of hurts inflicted by others. But Africa took things to a whole new level. We arrived in Uganda in 1981, just two short years after the downfall of dictator Idi Amin and his reign of terror. The country was in ruins. Shops were empty, roads were full of potholes, we could often hear shooting at night. There was disease, there was danger, there was death. But despite the state of the country, the believers we met shone like bright lights in the midst of darkness. They had been persecuted terribly, yet held on to their hope and faith in God. Rather than railing against God, they had a deep trust in Him despite the difficulties they had gone through.

## Pastor Charles Okwir

One of our dear friends throughout our years ministering in Africa was Pastor Charles Okwir. During Idi Amin's reign of terror, Idi Amin had allowed only Catholic and Anglican churches to function freely in Uganda; other denominations were outlawed. In response, the other churches went underground. Pastor Charles and his growing evangelical congregation evaded authorities by meeting illegally in different places each week. Unfortunately, it was not too long before the group was found by the local government.

One Sunday morning, two of Idi Amin's soldiers drove to Pastor Charles' village on the outskirts of Lira. At gunpoint, Pastor Charles was taken from his mud home and marched into the church, right up to the pulpit. Then one of the soldiers said, "Do you think you're the only one who can preach to people? Do you think you're the only one with power over people? I'll show you today who has the power." They pointed their guns at Pastor Charles and directed him out of the church and into their jeep. The soldiers drove out of Lira, taking him to a remote place where the soldiers used to execute people. Motioning for him to get out of the vehicle, the soldier pushed Pastor Charles forward and pointed the gun at his head.

Just before the soldier pulled the trigger, Pastor Charles asked, "May I say something to you before you kill me?"

"Go ahead," the soldier said.

Pastor Charles asked, "Are you going to kill me because I tell men to be faithful to their wives? Are you going to kill me because I encourage our people to pay their political tax? If you do, you're killing the wrong man. You will send me immediately to heaven." The soldier listened. Pastor Charles continued, "let me say one more thing to you before you kill me: Jesus Christ loves you."

As Pastor Charles spoke those final words of Jesus' love for his would-be murderer, the soldier slowly lowered the gun and said, "Get into the jeep."

Pastor Charles quickly responded to the order and the soldiers drove him to the police station. There, the soldier said to the commander in charge, "I want you to interrogate this man. I've never seen a man like him who wasn't afraid to die."

The soldier left the station and the interrogation began, but the policemen's grueling questions revealed nothing but a man who loved Jesus and the people he served. After three hours, the police told Pastor Charles he could return home.

Once Pastor Charles neared his church, he could hear people praying for him inside. Word had spread that he had been taken by Idi Amin's soldiers for execution, and the believers had quickly gathered together in response. Inside the church, faithful members were on their knees crying out in prayer for the release of their Pastor. Pastor Charles shouted, "Church, I'm here and I'm safe!" What ensued was no small celebration as his friends jumped up and down, hugging him and praising the Lord.

Pastor Charles could have let this traumatic experience scare him from following God's call on his life. He could have lived the rest of his life in fear. Instead, he decided to live boldly and continue ministering in that difficult time. This eventually led to a flourishing church movement, a school for children whose parents had died of AIDS or war, and a humanitarian ministry that impacted the region. His experiences of pain later helped him to minister to those escaping the terror of Joseph Kony and the so-called "Lord's Resistance Army" (LRA) that had devastated the region.

Rather than giving up in the midst of pain and trials, Pastor Charles continued to trust in God, continued to serve God, and became a channel of blessing to so many others in his country.

Gloria and I visited many villages during our six years of service in Uganda and we heard many similar stories of suffering and persecution. Yet what we witnessed were victorious churches with leaders whose faith remained steadfast, even at the threat of death. So great was the persecution during Idi Amin's reign of terror that many held their services outdoors, in the bush. One of the churches in the eastern part of Uganda literally hid behind rocks. At one point, I stood behind those very rocks where that church had gathered and began to imagine what it must have been like for them as they met in the dark of night.

It seemed like everyone had gone through some deep pain, some trauma – whether it was persecution for their faith, death because of malaria or some other disease, or lack of sanitation or malnutrition. Yet through it all their faith was so strong!

We noticed that many Ugandan Christians responded to suffering as the Psalmist did: "God is our refuge and strength, an ever present help in trouble. Therefore we will not fear, though the earth give way and the mountains fall into the heart of the sea" (Psalm 46:1-2). As the world around them churned with anxiety and violence, the faith of the church in Uganda was focused on its Saviour, knowing that their God would prevail:

> He makes wars cease to the ends of the earth.
> He breaks the bow and shatters the spear;
> he burns the shields with fire.
> He says, "Be still, and know that I am God;
> I will be exalted among the nations,
> I will be exalted in the earth (Psalm 46:9-10).

## The Sovereignty of God

One of the teachers at the Pentecostal Bible Training Centre in Mbale where we worked was Francis Manana. We became good friends with Francis and his wife Alice, spending a lot of time together at their apartment and in our home. They were expecting their first baby and, as the due date neared, I asked permission to drive them to the hospital when Alice was ready, as they did not have a vehicle of their own. When the day finally came Francis called and I quickly drove over to their apartment above the auto store to pick them up. Alice was quickly admitted to the Mbale Hospital, which, in 1983 was still in disrepair. Over the next few hours, the doctors realized the baby was not coming; the decision was made to deliver the baby via C-section. But there was a problem. The anesthetist was in the village many miles away. Someone would need to travel there to inform him of the situation and to bring him back. Because I had a vehicle, I offered to go at once.

Someone from the hospital accompanied me and we headed out on the back, dirt roads to the village of mud huts to fetch the doctor. Once he heard of the predicament, he jumped in the car and we returned to the hospital. They immediately prepared Alice for the surgery and soon after a healthy baby boy named Morrison Paul Manana was born. Francis and Alice's joy knew no bounds and we celebrated with them.

But then, tragedy struck. Over the next few days it became apparent that something was dreadfully wrong with Alice. The doctor told us the operating room must not have been sterile and, as a result, Alice had contracted an infection. We sadly watched Alice get weaker and weaker.

Though many believers prayed for her, she died. We were overwhelmed with sorrow and anger. Why did this have to happen? If Alice had been in Canada or the United States she would still be alive! Our missionary colleagues Wilbur Morrison (for whom baby Morrison had been named) and Ambrose Raymer were master carpenters. They spent the night making a coffin for Alice. Francis and asked me to drive him to their village to relay the sad news to Alice's family.

We returned to Mbale, where Alice had been taken to the church. Some of the women had washed her body, dressed her in one of Gloria's most beautiful dresses, and laid her body out on a cot. In Africa, because of the intense heat, if a person died in the morning they had to be buried before nightfall, and if they died at night they needed to be buried in the morning. Alice's body lay in the Pentecostal Assemblies of God (PAG) church all night as people came and paid their respects with many tears and sobs. In the morning, the funeral was held in that same PAG church, as people crowded in, and others peered through the windows and the doorway.

Alice's death confronted me with a disturbing question: *How could our good and loving God have allowed this to happen?* We know that God does allow pain into our lives but also that He can release us from its paralyzing emotional consequences if we will surrender our brokenness to Him. But why would He let a mother die during the birth of her first child? Perhaps my problem was that I had never been confronted with such a tragic circumstance in the lives of those whom I knew and loved personally.

I was deeply moved when Francis spoke at the funeral. At first, I could hardly believe what he was saying: he was thanking the doctors and nurses for their care of Alice! Why? It was their carelessness that caused her death! But as Francis continued to speak, I began to understand the high view of the sovereignty of God that sustained the Ugandan believers. They had lived through Idi Amin's nine-year reign of terror and through it all they had experienced the faithfulness of God. Francis was teaching me something that as a Westerner, I needed to hear. Simply put, it was this: God is good, whether life is fair or cruel, for that is His nature. His sovereignty over all circumstances can help us remain grateful and forgiving to people, even when they make tragic mistakes as the hospital staff did with Alice.

Francis's trust in God's sovereignty helped him through the service that day as Alice's coffin was carried from the church and down the road to her place of burial. His trust in a sovereign God continued to bolster him as his life now turned to the business of caring for his newborn baby.

Francis' story did not end there. Because he was willing to trust God and walk with Him into an uncertain future, he saw God's blessing on his life. He later remarried, the Lord gave them other children, he got his Doctorate in Ministry and had a wide-ranging teaching ministry, helping others who had also gone through great pain.

Often, we do not understand the way the Lord leads, but the key is to trust Him even when we do not understand, knowing that His love is pure and faithful.

## Questioning Why

Gloria and I experienced tragedies of our own while in Uganda. Gloria became pregnant with our fourth child, but she miscarried and had to go to a medical center in Nairobi, the capital of neighboring Kenya.

This was devastating to both of us and, like many, we questioned God and wondered if we could have done anything differently. "God, why did you allow this to happen?" "Maybe if we were in Canada the baby would have been born." But, ultimately, we had to learn to trust that God had a plan even in the midst of our own pain and hurt.

Perhaps you have experienced similar times of loss or pain. Maybe it was a miscarriage and the baby that you longed to hold is now gone. Or maybe you've experienced the tragedy of a child suddenly being taken from you or have lost a dearly loved family member or friend.

At times like these we can question "why" and begin to get angry with God. It just does not seem fair or right! Perhaps growing up you were told to "never question God" or "don't ask why." But one thing that has helped me in these moments is to realize that God is big enough for us to come to him with our questions. As parents, we are used to our children asking us questions. One of their favourites is, "but why?" – and they do it because they trust us as their care-givers. The greatest example of this is actually from Jesus Himself. When he was on the cross, in the agony of death and with the weight of the world's sin upon his shoulders, he cried out *"My God, My God, why have you forsaken me?"* (Matthew 27:46, emphasis mine).

Did you catch that? Jesus was asking the question we all ask – "Why?" If you dig a bit deeper you will see that Jesus was quoting Psalm 22, written by David. After going through one of the many difficult times in his life David had also asked the question, "Why?" It felt like God had forsaken him.

Despite his feelings, though, the reality was actually that God had *not* forsaken David, even though it sure felt like it at the time. And so we see David venting in the Psalm to God, crying out to Him. In fact, we see that over and over throughout the Psalms because that is what they are: expressions from the human heart to God. Some contain expressions of praise, while others deep cries of lament and despair.

> **God is big enough for us to come to Him with our questions.**

The amazing thing in Psalm 22 is that after pouring out his heart and doubts to God, *David actually begins to have his faith strengthened by the same God he was questioning!* He began to realize how near God was to the broken-hearted, how strong God was in the midst of his own pain. From verse 22 onwards he begins to declare how God has heard him and will deliver him and give him the strength to keep going on. By the time he finishes the Psalm, he realizes that God has not forsaken him, that God "has not despised or disdained the suffering of the afflicted one; he has not hidden his face from him" (verse 24).

Dr. Ajith Fernando, in his helpful book "The Call to Joy and Pain" puts it this way,

> Christians need not deny pain. At some time all Christians experience pain, discouragement, sorrow, and anger over wrong things and misfortunes that affect them. It is not helpful to deny these feelings. Often before we rejoice amidst pain we need to mourn or lament or express our pain in some such way.[24]

So, again, it's okay to grieve, to question, to recognize the pain that we are going through. But we don't stop there! We learn from David that it's in these times of doubt that we need to choose to run to God with our pain and questions – not run from him. And as we do, our crying out to him becomes an act of faith that will open the door for breakthrough, strength, and healing!

## No More Pain

It is human nature to question pain. Perhaps one of the reasons we do so is because we have an inner feeling that things are not as they should be. And indeed they're not – when God made this world it was perfect and he called it "good." But since sin entered the world, pain and death came with it. And so as long as we are on earth we will experience pain in some form or other. The Bible never promises a pain-free existence. Tragedies occur. Accidents take place. Sickness, death and disease are common-place. War, famines, and other natural disasters have been the experience of all humanity for thousands of years. The only promise we have of a life without pain is when we finally cross into eternity.

Revelation gives us hope, declaring that one day God will "wipe away every tear" and that there will be "no more death or sorrow or crying or pain." (Revelation 21:4, NLT).

But until then we live in a world where these things do take place. Jesus himself said, "in this world you will have trouble," but he continued, "take heart I have overcome the world" (John

16:33). He can give us His peace in the midst of tragedy, in the midst of pain. Sometimes the greatest sense of His presence is in those difficult times. In fact, thinking back to David and Psalm 22…the interesting thing is that the very next Psalm (the 23rd) is the famous one about the Lord being our Shepherd. There David declares his trust in God – that even though he might have to walk through the valley of the shadow of death, still he knows God is with him. Even though he is surrounded by enemies and fearful situations, God provides for him, anoints him, and comforts him. The Christian life is not one without pain or difficulty, but one where, even in the midst of pain and difficulty, we know we are not alone and that God is there with us.

It was during this time in Africa that the Lord had begun to impress on my mind the phrase, "My life is not my own." When we first arrived in Uganda and saw the broken condition of the country and her people, these words began to etch themselves into my spirit even more deeply. Over the next few months, as we drove the potholed roads of the country that had been called "the Pearl of Africa," and saw people dressed in tattered clothes and wearing the "spirit of despair" (Isaiah 61:3), a song began to come into my heart. Its words reflected the truth of Jeremiah 10:23: "I know that people's lives are not their own."

This song became the title track for our CD "Not My Own", and Scripture behind it the foundation for our ministry in Africa and beyond. Properly understood, "my life is not my own" is a biblical truth and a liberating thought in our "me-centered" culture. We can trust God to lead us and know it is good.

# Not My Own[25]

My life is not my own; it's in God's hand,
He'll order it the way that He deems best.
Therefore, I can trust Him and lean on His Word,
For, my life is not my own; it's in God's hand.

Calvary cost God the life of His Son,
And in that moment new life was begun,
For I was purchased and pardoned,
though not with gold coins,
But with the precious blood of Christ my Lord.

My life is not my own; it's in God's hand,
He'll order it the way that He deems best.
Therefore, I can trust Him and lean on His Word,
For, my life is not my own; it's in God's hand.

All who would follow the Christ of the cross
Soon will discover their life must be lost.
For in losing you find, and in dying you live;
Take up your cross, my friend, and follow Him.

My life is not my own; it's in God's hand,
He'll order it the way that He deems best. Therefore, I
can trust Him and lean on His Word,
For, my life is not my own; it's in God's hand.
— *Paul and Gloria Willoughby*

# Further Reflection

*"Why am I discouraged? Why is my heart so sad?*
*I will put my hope in God!*
*I will praise him again — my Savior and my God!"*
*(Psalm 43:5, NLT)*

1. What is your view of the sovereignty of God? (Job 42:1-6, 10; Psalms 37:1-11, 23-25; 73:21-28)?

2. Is it ever okay to question God or to express your doubts to Him?

3. Do you believe that one day God will "wipe away every tear?" Does that seem possible?

4. What part of the story of Francis Manana could you relate with the most? Why?

*"Even in hard times, God is trustworthy!"*

Go to **www.DontWasteYourPain.com/book** or scan the code on the right for videos and other resources related to this chapter!

# Chapter 10: Forgiveness and Freedom

In December 1987, just before Christmas, our family left Uganda and returned to Canada as I had been very sick and we could not figure out exactly what was wrong. Shortly after we arrived in Canada I was admitted to Sunnybrook Hospital in Toronto, as I had begun to break out in boils. The tropical disease specialist who cared for our missionaries, Dr. Philip Stuart, diagnosed me with a Staphylococcus (or "Staph") infection, for which I had to be put into isolation. Dr. Stuart also treated me for Schistosomiasis, also known as Bilharzia, a parasitic disease that had been in my body for five years – the result of baptizing believers in Lake Victoria in Uganda. Because the disease was so rare in Canada, he had to first obtain permission from the Federal Ministry of Health in Ottawa for the release of the medication. As a result, I spent a couple of weeks in the hospital dealing with these medical problems. Once I was discharged, it took some time to get back on my feet. I was so grateful for Gloria's care and leadership of our family during this time.

But physical sickness was not the only reason we came back to Canada. Once again, it was partly the result of my inability to deal with conflict that led to our return. During our last year in Africa, there had been some things said and done by fellow workers that left us hurt and wounded. I felt personally attacked and, unfortunately, responded the way I had always done – I kept it bottled up inside. I felt rejected, and rather than talk it through with my colleagues and face what could be difficult conversations and confrontation, decided to pack things up and head home.

As I look back on those years I see the repetition of the same mistakes, especially when it came to conflict. Maybe you have been there, too? You thought you had dealt with a pattern of behavior, but it keeps cropping up again. It's a human tendency to fall back on our natural reactions, especially if we have been abused in the past. With humility, we need to recognize that we are all works in progress and need grace day by day to keep growing and keep dealing with those areas with which we struggle.

Leaving Africa was extremely difficult for us. Not only was I worn down physically, I was also worn down emotionally. We loved Uganda and perhaps if we had been in a better space physically and emotionally we would have stayed and continued in the work there. Looking back it's easy to see that we should not make major life changes when we are unwell! But, gratefully, God is able to use even difficult times to teach us, to fashion us, and turn our brokenness into something beautiful. He can still make all things work together for our good!

During this time I also learned that I needed to grow in the area of forgiveness. Even though I felt like I had been the one that was wronged, since I was holding on to bitterness I would be the one that would suffer. It has been said, "unforgiveness is like drinking poison and expecting the other person to die."[26] It hurts you more than the other person. Rather than bringing you relief or healing, it only perpetuates the problem.

Many years later, as I began to grow in my recognition of the need for forgiveness, I met this former co-worker and we reconciled. You know, the funny thing is, he never even knew that he had hurt me with what he had said, or even why we left Africa! The pain that seems obvious to us, is not always clear to others.

Forgiving does not come easily to any of us. And the deeper we are wounded the harder it is to forgive. What can make it more difficult is that we often have to forgive many times throughout our life. In my own case, the pain of rejection brought memories of other pain in my life: the board member in Ottawa and, of course, the abuse I had endured as a child.

In chapter two I shared how I recommitted my life to Jesus and was filled with His Spirit. At that time with the awareness of the Spirit of God at work in my life in a new way, I began to realize the need to forgive my abuser. But how could I ever forgive him for the wounds he had inflicted upon me, for the pain he had caused? Forgiveness is never an easy process and is often one of the most difficult steps in our journey to healing.

## Jesus' Teaching on Forgiveness

Let's look at what the Scriptures say about forgiveness. Many of us learned the Lord's Prayer when we were children. Even if you did not, you may be familiar with it. Jesus said to His disciples,

"This, then, is how you should pray:
'Our Father in heaven, hallowed be your name,
your kingdom come, your will be done,
on earth as it is in heaven.
Give us today our daily bread.
*And forgive us our debts,*
*as we also have forgiven our debtors.*
And lead us not into temptation,
but deliver us from the evil one'
(Matthew 6:9-13, emphasis added).

Notice verse 12: "forgive us our debts as we also have forgiven our debtors." This suggests that the forgiveness extended to us is directly related to how much we are forgiving others who have sinned against us. Jesus states this truth even more clearly in the next two verses: "For if

> **The only way to overcome the bitterness that grows out of our brokenness is to forgive.**

you forgive other people when they sin against you, your heavenly Father will also forgive you. But if you do not forgive others their sins, your Father will not forgive your sins." God expects us to extend to others the love that He has freely given us. We have been forgiven by God's grace, which means we do not, nor could we ever earn or deserve His forgiveness (Ephesians 2:8, 9). As a result, we too are called to be gracious in freely forgiving others who have hurt us, *even though they don't deserve to be forgiven.*

This is not to say we should ignore horrific abuse or injustice. For example, crimes like child abuse must be confronted. The perpetrators cannot be allowed to continue destroying innocent children. But our focus in this book is not on what law enforcement should do, but on what we as individuals need to do. Our focus, and that of the Lord, is upon the brokenness caused by such abuse or other painful, soul-destroying experiences. God passionately desires to heal our brokenness because if these wounds are left unattended, the poisonous effects of fear, shame, and bitterness will continue to destroy both the victims and their families. That is why the Scripture warns so clearly against harboring bitterness: "See to it that no one falls short of the grace of God and that *no bitter root grows up* to cause trouble and defile many" (Hebrews 12:15, emphasis added). The person who suffers, as a result of bitterness, is not the one who caused the pain, but the victim who allows bitterness literally to eat them alive. Notice also that the consequences of bitterness are not restricted to the victim. They can and will "cause trouble and defile many" around them as well.

But how can bitterness be overcome? The actions that led to the abuse cannot be erased either from our personal histories or our hearts and minds. Nor can they be denied or ignored without perpetuating their corrosive effects – in some cases for generations. The only answer is forgiveness. The only way to overcome the bitterness that grows out of our brokenness is to do what Jesus said we must do: forgive the one who has sinned against us and wounded us. And the only way we can do this is by receiving God's undeserved and unrestricted forgiveness for our own sins.

Once we have done this, we begin to see the offender in a new light. We realize how undeserving all of us are of forgiveness, and yet Jesus, the only person who never sinned, has paid the price for our freedom with His own life. During His horrendous suffering on the cross, Jesus said, "Father, forgive them, for they do not know what they are doing" (Luke 23:34). Jesus set the example for all His followers and indeed for anyone who wants their brokenness healed. Only forgiveness can set you free from the paralyzing emotional pain of your brokenness. And only Jesus Christ can give you the power to forgive those who caused your pain.

In my own case, it took some time for me to come to the place of forgiveness. Even after I came to know the Lord and was filled with the Spirit, I would often see the man who abused me during my teen years, though we never talked about what had taken place. Then, in my early twenties, I knew it was time to confront him face to face and to forgive him. It was a very difficult thing for me to do, for up to that point I had lived in denial, trying to act as if the abuse had never happened. To forgive meant that I would have to face my pain and admit that something bad had taken place. I will never forget the day I approached him and looked him in the face. All I said to him was, "I forgive you." He looked at me for a moment, then turned and walked away without saying a word. His unwillingness to acknowledge his sin or show any sign of remorse or guilt left me feeling exposed. My emotions were already raw, and that felt like another blow on top of my wounded soul. But in my heart, I had forgiven him, and that was what really mattered.

We have to face the fact that sometimes even though we are willing to forgive the person, they may not be willing to admit their mistakes or sins. When that happens we are tempted to say, "See, it's no use! I knew they'd do that!" Our hearts can begin to harden again. Old wounds can re-open. At that stage, we need to just leave the results to God, knowing that we have tried to walk in obedience. Remember, forgiveness is not just about them – it's also about our own healing and freedom. And we cannot be free when we are holding onto the hurts of the past.

Forgiveness is never easy. But it is necessary to bring healing to your own soul and to enable you to minister healing to others as well.

## What Is Forgiveness?

Although forgiveness is essential, it can be a very difficult thing to do. Sometimes forgiving is extra hard because we misunderstand what it is really all about. When we speak of forgiveness, it does **not** mean the following:

First, it does <u>not</u> mean what they did was **right**. Whether it was abuse, or betrayal, or something else, that sinful thing is still wrong. When Margaret forgave her brother (in chapter one) for the horrible abuse against her, it did not mean those actions were any less horrific. What it did was *set her free* from the pent up anger and bitterness that was eating her away on the inside. In the same way, when Maury forgave his step-father, it did not mean what had happened could be shrugged off or forgotten, but it allowed Maury to experience the freedom that he so desperately needed.

Second, forgiveness does <u>not</u> negate the **consequences** of an action. If a drunk driver kills someone you love, you have a choice to forgive them. If you choose to forgive, that does not mean they are absolved of their responsibility. They still need to face the law. Perhaps they will spend years in jail for their deed. But, here is the key: you can choose to extend forgiveness to them so that you yourself *are not locked in a prison* of bitterness.

Third, forgiveness does <u>not</u> mean you have to **trust** them. If an abuser asks for forgiveness, you can extend it to them. But that does not mean that you need to trust them in the future. If a business partner was inept and caused millions of dollars of losses, you could forgive them – but you would not necessarily go back into business with them again!

Related to this is the idea of boundaries. You have taken the step to forgive the person who hurt you, but you still need boundaries in your life. In an abusive relationship, you can forgive the abuser, but that does not mean you go back to them or always let them back into your life. This is difficult, but it means setting boundaries so that you do not open yourself up to greater hurts in the future. This does not mean building a wall around your heart, but rather it's a recognition that others are not perfect. So you can walk in love, but still have the courage to say "no." Perhaps you need an accountability partner who will help you to say "no," especially if the one who has caused you pain tries to manipulate you in order to exert their power over you again.

Fourth, forgiveness does not mean you '**feel**' like forgiving them or that you will suddenly 'like' the person. As we will see in the next story, forgiveness often starts as an act of the will. You may not feel like it, but you know you have to forgive. The amazing thing is, that as you do, you experience healing on the inside as well.

What forgiveness means is that you are *letting go of your right to get even*. This is the example God gives us. He is perfect and He could choose to get even with us for all the many sinful things we have done. But He chooses to let go of His right to get even – that is what His grace is all about! And since we have been forgiven by God, we also need to extend this forgiveness to others. That is why this is the one thing

> **Forgiveness is letting go of your right to get even**

that Jesus emphasized after giving His famous teaching we call the Lord's Prayer. The reason He highlights forgiveness is because He truly wants us to walk in freedom and wholeness and He knows that unforgiveness will keep us bound and locked up, unable to experience the full blessings God has for our lives.

## Forgiving Yourself

While it is common to struggle with forgiving others, sometimes we also need to learn to forgive ourselves. Wrong choices we have made, bridges we have burned, people we have sinned against – all of these can contribute to our own pain. There were many times during the years I hosted *Nite Lite Live* that women would call in, weeping because they could not forgive themselves for having had an abortion. In situations like this, the devil weighs us down with guilt and we think, "God could never forgive me!" But the truth is that when we come to Jesus in humility and confess our sins, He can forgive us – no matter what we have done! The apostle John put it this way, "If we confess our sins, he is faithful and just and will forgive us our sins and purify us from all unrighteousness" (1 John 1:9). The thief on the cross not only received forgiveness, but also the amazing promise that he would be with Jesus in paradise (see Luke 23:43). Paul the apostle had persecuted the church, hunting down Christians and approving of their deaths. Because of his past, he went so far as calling himself "the worst of sinners" (1 Timothy 1:15). But despite that, he was willing to receive God's grace and mercy, to put his old life behind him, and to walk in this new life with the freedom that only Jesus could give!

## The Freedom of Forgiveness

One of the guests we had on 100 Huntley Street that exemplified forgiveness more than almost anyone else was Corrie ten Boom. Corrie's life was made famous in the book and movie, "The Hiding Place." She lived in the Netherlands during the outbreak of World War 2 and witnessed the Nazi's invading her homeland. When they began their anti-Semitic propaganda and attacks, Corrie and her family hid dozens of Jews in a secret room in their home.

Eventually, they were betrayed and Corrie and her family were sent to prison where her father soon died. Then she and her sister Betsie were transferred to the Ravensbruck concentration camp. It was a horrific place, with brutal beatings, starvation, humiliation, and death. Slowly, in that cruel and inhumane environment, she watched her sister Betsy die. Just two weeks after Betsie's passing, Corrie was released (later she learned it was a clerical error. A few days after she was sent home, everyone Corrie's age was sent to the gas chambers to die).

No one would fault Corrie if she had come out bitter and angry at God. But instead, she began to testify of God's goodness, His love and power even in the midst of horror. As Betsie had said before her death, "There is no pit so deep, that God's love is not deeper still."

But it was not easy. Corrie told of one time, just a few years after the war, she had been sharing on God's forgiveness in a church in Germany. After the message a man came up – Corrie recognized him as a guard at Ravensbruck, one of the men that had beaten and humiliated her and her sister Betsie.

He had done evil and inhumane things – things that would haunt him for the rest of his life. It was so hard for him to believe that God could be merciful to him after all that he had done, but perhaps he thought, "if a fellow human could forgive me, maybe God could forgive me too." Though he did not recognize Corrie at first, he asked if God really had forgiven him and if she would forgive him too.

How could she forgive a man who had tortured and abused so many? Even though she had just finished a message on forgiveness, she was momentarily paralyzed. What could she do? She said she remembered that forgiveness was not a feeling – no, it is an act of the will. Even though she did not want to forgive this man, did not feel like forgiving him, she knew that was what Jesus was calling her to do.

With a quick prayer, she reached out to shake his outstretched hand, and as she did so a mighty wave of God's love flowed over her. "I had never known God's love so intensely as I did then" she later testified.[27]

## Set yourself free!

What Corrie did was not an easy thing. But imagine if she had chosen to withhold forgiveness. In one sense, she would have been physically free, but emotionally still in the concentration camp, still in prison.

But, you may ask, how can I ever forgive that person for what they have done? May I gently ask in response, how can you not forgive them? Why in the world would you still want to remain under their power? For that is what unforgiveness does – it ties us to the sinner and keeps us under their influence. It loads us down with bitterness and anger, memories that swirl like storms in our hearts. Do we really want to live like that? Don't we want to be free from such chains? As Lewis Smedes so aptly said, "To forgive is to set a prisoner free and discover that the prisoner is you."[28]

But how can we do that? The truth is that in our own strength it is almost impossible. We need God's help. Like Corrie, you may not 'feel' like forgiving. But forgiveness is not a feeling, it's an act of the will. If you are struggling with this, I encourage you to go to the Lord in prayer. Say something like this: *"Lord God, I don't feel like forgiving (the person's name), but I know you want me to and I know I need to. Please help me to forgive them. I am willing to be made willing to forgive them. Please give me your grace to forgive them, just as you have forgiven me. In Jesus Name Amen."*

It is my prayer that you will take this step. It may take some time, maybe weeks of praying a prayer like the one above. But as you ask God to help you and make you willing to forgive, you will be brought to a place of new life and peace and hope!

# Further Reflection

*"But when you are praying, first forgive anyone you are holding a grudge against, so that your Father in heaven will forgive your sins, too." (Mark 11:25, NLT)*

1. Have you ever had the experience of being forgiven when you didn't deserve it? What were the circumstances? How did it feel? How did it affect your life (Ephesians 2:8-10; 1 John 1:6, 7)?

2. Why is it important to understand what forgiveness does *not* mean?

3. What do you think of the quote, "to forgive is to set a prisoner free and discover that the prisoner is you"? Have you ever been in the 'prison' of unforgiveness?

4. If you had been in Corrie's position, would you have been able to forgive?

5. Why is forgiveness so important in releasing us to God's purpose for our lives (Psalms 32:1-7; Matthew 6:14, 15; 18: 21-35; Ephesians 4:26, 27, 30-32)?

*"Forgiveness is essential for true freedom!"*

Go to **www.DontWasteYourPain.com/book** or scan the code on the right for videos and other resources related to this chapter!

# Chapter 11: Look Beyond Your Own Brokenness

After we returned from Uganda we pastored for a number of years at New Life Assembly in Belle River. During these years we were privileged to work with Tim and Bonnie Atkins. Tim was our associate pastor, a very capable and gifted man, and Bonnie, who served as the church secretary, was extremely efficient, gentle, and compassionate. Coming back from Africa I had been discouraged and felt like a failure. But with his great sense of humor, Tim helped me to learn to laugh again—and there was lots of laughter! Together, Tim and Bonnie were a great team and helped us immeasurably in our six years of ministry at Belle River.

During that time we saw many people come to the Lord and the church had a time of growth. Of course, there were also challenges, but through it all tremendous personal relationships were built, and the church caught a real passion for missions.

In our fifth year of ministry at New Life, our church gave us the gift of a four-week mission trip. Our plan was to visit friends in East Africa and to see how the churches were doing.

But the Lord had some slightly different plans. A few years previous, an international student from India, Anita Ninan, had attended our church. She had come to Canada to do her Master of Arts in Communications at the University of Windsor, and was staying with a family near the church. Because of our time overseas we understood some of the culture shock Anita was going through and were able to help her adjust. Over time, we formed a very close friendship with her that continues to this day.

When Anita heard the news that we were heading to Africa — by this time she had graduated with her Master's degree and was back in India—she said, "Pastor Paul, you and Gloria have to visit India since you'll be so close in Uganda!" She urged us to meet her father who, desiring to communicate the gospel in creative ways, had founded the Centre for Communication Skills. Both Gloria and I agreed it would be good to meet him, so we planned to spend two weeks in Bangalore, India with her family, and then two weeks in East Africa.

Before we left we had a talk with the Missions Director of our denomination, sensing that this was greater than just a short-term trip. Was there an opportunity to reengage with the work we had previously done in Uganda? "Well," he said, "to be honest, we're not going to send anyone to Uganda as the work there is going strong…but if any opportunity arises in India, that may be a possibility!"

Having spent six years in post–Idi Amin Uganda, where the sound of gunfire at night and the sight of skulls piled high in the Luwero Triangle outside of Kampala was not abnormal, we thought that we had seen it all. However, when we landed in India I had a serious case of culture shock! The masses of people, the lack of hygiene, the disparity between the rich and poor, and the odor of the rivers all hit me like a ton of bricks. That was not the only thing that hit me – food poisoning I picked up on the second day in the country made the already pungent smells more than I could take. Despite how I was feeling, Anita was so hospitable, welcoming us into her family's two-bedroom apartment where she, her parents, Dr. George and Pamela Ninan, and her mother's sister, Aunty Joyce Rodericks, lived. Unlike me, Gloria did not feel any culture shock whatsoever; she absolutely loved India. When I felt better after a couple of days, they showed us around the city. We spoke and sang eleven times in fifteen days at various churches, bible colleges, and parachurch ministries. But truth be told, I could not wait to leave India and was grateful to board our plane for East Africa.

As the plane made its descent into Nairobi, it felt as if we were entering the Garden of Eden, so great was the contrast to me.

We made our way through Kenya to a missionary retreat centre where we spent a couple of days with friends. Then we traveled on to Lira in northern Uganda, where something very unusual happened. Pastor Charles Okwir's wife Margaret was serving us breakfast in their small mud hut as we all sat on homemade wooden chairs. Both Gloria and I were overwhelmed by their love, and tears began to flow from my eyes as they asked, "brother Paul, sister Gloria when are you returning to Uganda?" Just then, deep in my spirit, the Lord spoke so clearly: "Paul, I don't need you here, but if you are willing, I need you in India." At that moment culture shock ceased to be an issue and in my heart I responded, "Lord, if you want us to go to India, then that's where we'll go!" Later when Gloria and I were alone, I shared with her what had happened. She was excited at the possibility of ministering among the people of India. After spending time in prayer and talking with the missions director about the opportunity, we decided to pursue what God had spoken to my heart.

Upon returning to Canada our dear friend David Mainse suggested we use the Crossroads children's program *Kingdom Adventure*, which was created and produced by his son-in-law, Bruce Stacey, as values-based programming for India's children. Through the generosity of several Canadian friends and churches, we were able to raise the financing and purchase the show's broadcast rights for India.

Things fell into place quickly and within a year we were back in India, working alongside Dr. George and Pamela Ninan in the Centre for Communication Skills in Bangalore.

## India

It took some time and we had a number of hoops to jump through, but eventually we were able to get the *Kingdom Adventure* children's program on a government television channel that was seen in all cities throughout India. The program's godly values and message of hope touched countless lives throughout the country.

Our four years in India opened our eyes to further levels of suffering and injustice. We learned, for example, about the caste system which, still held millions captive to its way of life. Although caste discrimination was formally abolished, it still dictates almost every facet of life: what job you do, where you can eat, where you can go to school, and so on. Violence against the lower caste was a regular occurrence.

We also were introduced to the terrible reality of human trafficking, exploitation, and the tragedy of the *devadasis*, who often became temple prostitutes.

> The devadasi practice is one in which low-caste girls, as young as five or six, are "married" to a Hindu [deity] and sexually exploited by temple patrons and higher caste individuals. The term devadasi is a Sanskrit word, which literally translates to "female slave of God."[29]

Swami Harshananda in his book, *All About Hindu Temples*, describes the function of the *devadasi* in this way:

> This system was opposed by the Brahmans. However, due to the pressure of the kings and noblemen it came to stay. The girls chosen to become *devadasi* would be married to the deity in the temple in a ceremonial way. Their main duties consisted of cleaning the temple, fanning the image, carrying lights, singing and dancing before the deity and devotees and so on. The system might have started some time during the third century A.D. It soon degenerated into prostitution, thanks to the notorious human weaknesses.[30]

As we would later find out, this was one of the things the great missionary to India, Amy Carmichael, devoted her life to – rescuing little girls from a life of degradation and abuse.

This practice weighed heavily on our hearts, as did the plight of child-labourers, migrant workers, and the Dalits (formerly the "untouchables") whose lives were worth very little in the eyes of many. Who would show them their worth in the sight of God? Who would tell them that the One who touched lepers and loved the outcast, loved them too? At the time we had no idea that God would one day open the door for us to bring His message of hope and healing to these very people.

## Look Beyond Yourself

One of the lessons we were learning was the need to look beyond ourselves to the pain that others are going through. So often we can become consumed with our own hurts and misery. While my own hurts were very real, what I saw in India was pain and injustice on a whole new level. As I became aware of the great needs all around me, I realize that the hurts I had gone through had actually prepared me to minister to those also experiencing great pain.

This does not mean we ignore or minimize our own pain. But when we begin to reach out to others who are hurting an amazing thing happens: we ourselves receive joy, blessing, and fulfillment. This in turn helps find healing and restoration in our own lives, gives us passion, and even fills us with a new purpose for living.

We are like the little boy that was brought to Jesus when all he had was five loaves and two fish. But when he gave it all away to the Lord, instead of leaving empty, he left with more than he came with! Not only was

> **One of the lessons we were learning was the need to look beyond ourselves to the pain that others were going through.**

everyone else fed, but he was too! He and the others left with more than enough! Imagine if he had kept his food to himself, more aware of his own hunger pangs than the needs of those around him, what would he have missed out on?

So we see this principle at work – when we give, even if it is out of our pain, God will pour back into our lives, often in miraculous ways.

In Elijah's day, there was a severe famine in the land. Many were suffering and in need. God had provided for Elijah, guiding him to a brook with water and feeding him in a miraculous way by sending ravens to bring him food! But one day even the river dried up and the ravens stopped coming. God told him to go and visit a widow and ask her for help. Maybe Elijah thought he was being sent to a wealthy woman or someone with a lot of resources. But when he arrived at the spot he found a poor widow who had run out of all her resources. She had thought, "I'm going to make this and die!" (see 1 Kings 17:12). She could have been thinking, "What kind of person would ask me to share with them when I myself am in need? What about me? What about my own needs?" That's the usual human response. But what do we see in this story? The widow actually took a step of faith and agreed to make food for Elijah. When she did, God honoured her faith by performing a miracle so that she was provided for as well!

What she did was so amazing that Jesus highlighted this widow's actions in Luke 4:26. Looking beyond our own pain to the hurts and needs of others often opens up doors of possibility and of God's provision. Later, Jesus shared this principle: it is more blessed to give than to receive (see Acts 20:35).

The key here is to apply this principle to our own emotional wounds, our brokenness, and the healing process. Yes, we need to work through our own pain, but we cannot camp there. We need to recognize our hurts, deal with our past, but not fixate on them. We bring them to Jesus and allow him to take us and use us, broken as we are. As we do, not only will we see others healed, but we will find great healing as well!

## Martyrdom And Forgiveness

In the midst of all the pain we witnessed, there was one tragedy that really hit home to us. During those years we met and became friends with an Australian family who went to the same boarding school as our children, in the beautiful hill station town of Ootacamund. Hebron was a great school set 7,500 feet above sea level in the rather small town affectionately nicknamed, "Ooty." Over 100 years ago a small church was started in town by the legendary cricketer and missionary C. T. Studd. The likes of Amy Carmichael and other missionaries would often escape the sweltering heat by heading to these hills.

We became friends with many of the other parents whose children attended the school, along with Graham and Gladys Staines, Australian missionaries in Orissa. Their older children, Esther and Philip, were in the younger grades at Hebron School while their youngest child Timothy still lived at home with them in Orissa. At different times of the year, parents would come and stay near the school for special activities that lasted up to a week. It was during these visits that I got to know Graham and to sense his heart for the people that he and Gladys worked among. Graham was an ordinary man like me, wanting to make a difference in a difficult place. No one knew at the time the great price he and his family would pay as followers of Jesus Christ.

During our last few months in India we made a video promo of Hebron School. Part of the filming included a short clip featuring Graham and Gladys's son, Philip. Only ten years of age with blond hair and a cute grin, Philip said, "I really like Hebron. The food is good and the teachers are nice. I'm glad to be here." It was a short segment, fun and innocent. I had no way of knowing that it would be one of the last taped pieces of Philip.

After our return to Canada, Gloria and I were asked to speak at Summit Pacific College in Abbotsford, British Columbia. We got up early one morning and I picked up the *Globe and Mail* newspaper that had been delivered to our hotel room. My heart dropped as I read the headline: "Missionary and Sons Burned Alive in India." Horrified, I scanned the article and saw Graham's name along with those of his two sons, Philip and Timothy. According to the article, they had been locked in their jeep by Hindu radicals who then doused the vehicle with gasoline and set it on fire. The harsh reality of how horribly broken we are as human beings began to sink in, like never before. Kneeling by the side of the hotel bed, I wept. Ruben Banarjee reporting in *The Times* of India on February 8, 1999, described the scene:

> Even in death they were inseparable. Charred beyond recognition and reduced to fragile frames of ashes, the three bodies lay clinging to each other in what must have been a vain attempt to protect each other and escape the mob. But on the fateful night of January 22–23 in the wilderness of Manoharpur village in the sleepy rural outback of Orissa's Keonjhar district, nothing worked for the hapless father and his two sons. Having surrounded them from all sides, a murderous crowd set on fire the old four-wheel-drive Willy's station wagon in which the three had retired for the night. The beastly act done, Australian-born Christian missionary Graham Stewart Staines, 58, and his two sons, Phillip, 10, and Timothy, 7, were put to sleep forever. No sooner had its macabre mission been completed than the mob melted away in the darkness as the flames that had leapt skywards simmered. But the heat generated by the senseless killings and the outrage stoked are far from ebbing days after the incident.[31]

What happened next was truly amazing. Remarkably, Gladys Staines rose above the pain of her loss and demonstrated the ways of her loving Lord Jesus Christ, the living God. She openly forgave those who killed her husband and two sons.[32]

So foreign was this response to injustice and tragedy in India that people began to flock to Gladys; she became like a saint to the nation. India's reaction to Gladys Staines forgiving those who had taken her husband and sons from her was not the work of a saint, but of a humble and obedient follower of the Lord Jesus. He made it clear to His disciples:

> You have heard that it was said, 'Love your neighbor and hate your enemy.' But I tell you, love your enemies and pray for those who persecute you, that you may be children of your Father in heaven. He causes his sun to rise on the evil and the good, and sends rain on the righteous and the unrighteous (Matthew 6:43-45).

Jesus not only taught this, but he practiced it from the cross, forgiving those that were crucifying him. We also see in Acts chapters 6 and 7 the story of Stephen, the Church's first martyr. While an enraged mob was in the act of stoning him, he fell to his knees, and with his last breath he cried out with a loud voice: "Lord, do not hold this sin against them" (Acts 7:60).

Stephen in the early church, Corrie ten Boom, and Gladys Staines were doing what Jesus asks us all to do: Forgive those who hurt us, not because they deserve it, but because that is what God does for us. That is what Jesus did for me and you. We are no more worthy of His forgiveness than the mob that murdered Graham Staines and his two boys. Once we lay hold of this truth, there is nothing that can stand in the way of our restoration to wholeness, regardless of what we have suffered.

Reflecting on his own difficult journey overcoming suffering, noted Methodist missionary to India, E. Stanley Jones said, "If God … cares for the leper, the outcast, the blind, and if his heart is like that gentle heart that broke upon the cross, then he can have my heart without reservation and without question. For then, when

He has my heart, he is able to heal my heart of any damage the world may do to it."[33]

If Gladys had been focused on herself and her own pain, she never would have been able to say such words or to continue in ministry.

Hebrews says that Jesus, "for the joy set before him endured the cross" (Hebrews 12:2). Jesus was enabled to look beyond the pain and see something greater: the transformed lives that would take place because of what He was going through. Now, obviously, none of us are Jesus and we do not suffer for others in the same way Jesus suffered for us. But what we can learn is that when we look at the pain that others are going through, God gives us the grace to endure our own pain. And as we serve others and minister God's love to them, we begin to move beyond our hurts. Focusing on ourselves does not bring the freedom we desire. Laying down our lives and serving others paradoxically brings healing to our own hearts as well.

# Further Reflection

*One person gives freely, yet gains even more; another withholds unduly, but comes to poverty. (Proverbs 11:24)*

1. Are you aware of the pain that is around you?

2. How could Gladys Staines forgive those that killed her husband and two sons?

3. Why is it important to look beyond ourselves?

*"Healing accelerates when we look beyond ourselves!"*

Go to **www.DontWasteYourPain.com/book** or scan the code on the right for videos and other resources related to this chapter!

# Chapter 12: It's Not Too Late

In early January 1998, Gloria and I were in Ooty visiting friends originally from Denmark. One night during our stay I had a dream in which the Lord spoke to my heart: "Do not be afraid. Up to now you have seen what you can do. As a child puts his hand in his father's hand and walks with him, put your hand in mine and walk with me. Trust me, walk with me, and I will show you what I can do through you." When I woke up, I remembered clearly what the Lord had said in the dream and later that morning shared it with Gloria. It reminded me of Isaiah 41:13: "For I am the Lord your God, the one who takes hold of your right hand and says to you, Fear not; I will help you!"

The Lord was preparing me, for what I did not yet know but sensed it was connected to the vision of a late-night television show that I had so many years before. A few months later, on the evening of June 7, 1998, I was taking some time to pray in our two-bedroom apartment in Bangalore. As I knelt by the bed in the spare room I sensed the Lord speaking to my heart again. I wrote these words in my prayer journal: "I don't know how, I don't know when, but I sense the Lord is going to reconnect us to Crossroads."

Three weeks after that evening of prayer, I was on my way to the train station to pick up tickets for the train to Chennai when I sensed that check again in my spirit, telling me to cancel the train trip and stay home. I canceled the tickets. A couple of days later, on July 9, 1998, I was sitting in our apartment when the telephone rang. It was David Mainse from Crossroads. "Paul, have you heard we've got our twenty-four-hour TV station?"

No, I had not heard. David began to share his excitement that Crossroads had been granted a license by the Canadian Radio-Television and Telecommunications Commission for a new twenty-four-hour television station. He asked whether I would be interested in freelancing with the new station. I told him that I was but needed to check with our Head Office to find out if they would release me. We finished our conversation and I went into our bedroom, got on my knees by the side of the bed, amazed at what the Lord seemed to be doing, and began to worship. Over the next few days, I made some telephone calls to our Director, and he released me for seven weeks to return to Crossroads. I was excited at the prospect of going to work with David again! The final few weeks seemed to go by quickly as we said our good-byes to the many dear friends we had made in India during our last four years. The India chapter of our lives seemed to come to a close, and the dream of producing and hosting a late-night television show began stirring in my heart once again.

## Nite Lite Live

Twenty years had passed since I had worked with David Mainse at *100 Huntley Street*, and here I was, back where I had started. This time though, I felt that I was ready for late-night ministry. David, being the visionary that he was, had already started a late-night call-in show back in the early '80s. It was called, *Nite Lite Live* and was hosted by various Toronto-area pastors each night. The show had been very effective and David often called it "the best fishing hole in Canada!" Financial restraints had kept *Nite Lite Live* off the air in the '90s, but this was about to change with the coming of Crossroads Television System (CTS), which would give Crossroads its own twenty-four-hour channel.

When we first arrived back in Canada I worked as an associate producer for one of the programs at CTS. After a few months I then transitioned back to helping with guesting on *100 Huntley Street,* and, along with Nizar Shaheen, as producer-host of

*Let There Be Light*, a thirty-minute pre-taped program that aired once a week.

Shortly afterward I was also asked to host *Nite Lite Live* once a week. Then in late 2001, David asked if I would produce the program, though others would continue to host it throughout the week. The following June I had the strong sense in my spirit that David was going to ask me to also host the show full time, meaning I could finally realize the vision God had given me in my mid-twenties of producing and hosting a late-night call-in program, reaching out to the nation.

A month later David asked me to meet him. He was quick to get to the point. "Paul, I'd like you to produce and host *Nite Lite Live* full time. Take some time to think about it. You would no longer be working on *100 Huntley Street*; your full time would be given to *Nite Lite Live*." I shared with David what the Lord had spoken to me two months earlier and said, "I'm ready to begin."

September 9, 2002, I began to produce and host *Nite Lite Live* full time, with David Kwan as my associate producer, going to air from 2:00 to 4:30 a.m. I eventually invited Neil Cole to join the *Nite Lite Live* team. He had been the Ontario representative of *Freedom in Christ Canada* and had a real gift for teaching the *Freedom in Christ* material by Dr. Neil Anderson. Besides doing a teaching segment on *Nite Lite Live* each night that worked through this valuable series, Neil Cole was also my trusted call-screener. Early each morning at 1:30 a.m. we would meet for prayer before going to air, where we sought the help of the Lord for that program. (A link to some of his excellent teaching segments can be found on our website).

It was a privilege to encounter people at their point of deepest need as well as to inspire hope by sharing the testimonies of people who had walked through pain and come out the other side. *Nite Lite Live* truly helped people encounter Jesus during the darkest hours of the night when they were walking through the darkest times of their lives. There are too many stories to tell from those years, so let me share just a few that really stood out to me.

## Glamour, Guilt...and Grace!

One of our guests was Tressa Lemky, former model and Miss Canada contestant. Despite her achievements and outward beauty she struggled for years with low self-esteem and shame. Wrong choices had led to broken relationships, bulimia, and the pain of abortion. Yet one day she discovered that God could extend His grace to her and she found the hope and healing that is available in Jesus! She is now an author and speaker, and leads the ministry "The Esther Touch."[34]

## Discovering Hope for Depression

Scott Forbes was a high-achieving leader in his workplace, yet things came crashing down on him as he suddenly spiraled into depression. On *Nite Lite Live* he talked about the signs of depression in men and the importance of learning to talk about it and deal with it – something that us men don't often do well! His wisdom on the steps to both recognize and overcome depression really resonated with our viewers and continues to impact thousands of listeners.

## The Man with the Gun

One night a male caller from a rural town called during the program, deeply troubled. He said he had a gun and was going to harm his daughter. I tried to keep him talking on the line as long as possible while, as per our protocol, our call screener took down his phone number and called 911. Police were quickly dispatched and were able to locate the man so that within 1-2 hours the situation was diffused, and the child unharmed.

## Hope in Hospitals

I remember once I was speaking at a banquet, when afterward a young woman came up to me and began to share how much she enjoyed watching Nite Lite, and that in fact she, along with the other nurses on her floor watched Nite Lite on their individual breaks because they found it so helpful to them in their work of caring for the sick.

Another time I had travelled to St. Catharines, Ontario, to visit one of our faithful prayer partners from the midnight crew at 100 Huntley Street, who was battling cancer. As I got off the elevator at his floor a nurse in uniform looked at me quizzically and asked, "are you Paul Willoughby?" When I said 'yes', she choked up and began to weep saying, "you'll never know how much you have helped me!" Unable to control her sobbing, she walked away down the hall. I never did find out the rest of her story! But it underscored the fact that so many were going through such difficult times in their lives – and that Jesus could bring hope in the midst of the pain.

## First Nations, Second Chance

Another night a man from Toronto called for the first time. He had been surfing the channels and came upon the program where the question on the screen was, "Is life worth living?" He said he wasn't even sure he believed in God from all the abuse he received at Residential Schools. Prior to that he had seen his own mother shot and killed. As an adult, he led a rough life and even became a mule for the mafia in Toronto. He acknowledged that life was not worth living, that he planned to drive his car to northern Ontario, to a remote area, row his canoe to the middle of the lake, tie weights around his leg and drown himself. He said, "no one would ever know. No one would ever miss me." As we talked further, I shared that Jesus truly loved him and, that though hard to believe, God had a plan for his life. It was a longer call than normal that night, and as we talked further I asked if he would like to open his heart and life to Jesus, to give God a chance to deal with the pain he was experiencing. He agreed, and so I led him, line by line in a simple prayer of surrender and opening his heart and life to Jesus. After the call, I asked him to stay on the line because I wanted to call him later that day to follow up on our conversation. We later met up at a Tim Hortons where I was able to pray with him further and connect him with a Church and Pastor in his area.

## A Caller Named Pattie

A number of times Pattie Mallette, Justin Bieber's mother, called *Nite Lite*. She often said, "If it wasn't for *Nite Lite* I would not make it through the night!"

After a few calls and sharing a bit of her story, I invited her to be a guest on the show. So on July 19, 2006, I had Pattie Mallette on *Nite Lite* for the first time. It was one of the most honest and open interviews of anyone I had ever had on the program. The theme for the night was "Are you unable to bear the emptiness & pain you feel?" (You wouldn't believe how many people are up in the middle of the night, not able to deal with their pain – trying to drown it, cover it, unable to sleep). Pattie shared about her tragic childhood: a dad who had left the family, the terrible abuse she went through as a young girl, and how she tried to drown the emptiness through alcohol, drugs, and relationships. Finally, at the age of seventeen she could not take the pain anymore and planned to take her life – but failed in the attempt. As a result, she was admitted to a psychiatric ward and felt that she was trapped, alone, and more hopeless than ever. Despite the darkness; however, there was one ray of light. The director of the local youth centre, who had known Pattie, heard of her situation and would often come and visit her, letting her know that God still loved her and still had a plan for her life. He challenged her, "you say you've got nothing to live for. Since you've got nothing left to lose…why not give God a chance?"

At first hesitatingly she began to pray, "God, if it's not too late, if I haven't gone too far, would you forgive me and give me another chance?" She immediately sensed God's presence and had a vision of Him pouring His immense love into her heart. She felt such freedom! Suddenly she cried out, "God, you're real, you're real!" Pattie had her ups and downs after this experience, but through it all she knew that God was real, had forgiven her, and had a purpose for her life. Sometime later she gave birth to a little boy named Justin who seemed to have an incredible gift for music. When he was just twelve years old Pattie decided to put one of his videos on YouTube and the rest is pop culture history. Pattie's story reminds us that no matter the state of our own brokenness, God can reach through and redeem it for His purpose!

## Dreams, Detours, and Destinies

It's always so amazing and humbling to look back and reflect on all the lives that were changed, saved, encouraged and transformed through *Nite Lite Live*. So many who were helped to take just another step, to keep going another day. The dream I had been given years before in Tweed had become a reality – though it had taken so much longer than I had initially anticipated!

Sometimes we're guilty of trying to rush God's plan for our lives. I know that when I first had the vision for a late-night program that would reach the broken and hurting I thought it would come to pass right away. But it took over 25 years for me to see it fulfilled. In the meantime I had to learn many important lessons, I needed to be equipped with the tools and experience – and character – that would enable me to minister with compassion to those that were hurting.

Sometimes God may give us a dream or a passion, but we're not ready for it yet. So He takes us on a journey to shape our character, to give us a different perspective and deeper compassion. He reworks the "detours" of our lives and makes them fit together into something that actually can work out for our good.

I want to remind you of the Scripture from Romans 8 that says, "we know that God causes everything to work together for the good of those who love God" (Romans 8:28, NLT). We like to quote that verse – but, to be honest, it's sometimes hard to see how God can turn our pain into something good, isn't it?

My wife is a great cook and the house is often filled with the smell of something baking. The strange thing (to me) is that you can put all kinds of "untasty" things into a cake, and yet it will turn out delicious! Gloria will measure out the right amount of flour, salt, and baking soda, as well as the really essential stuff – sugar and chocolate chips. If you were to try a spoonful of flour or a teaspoon of baking soda, you'd spit it right out! But put it together, mix it around, and place it in the intense heat of an oven...and out comes something that smells and tastes amazing!

You know, life is something like that. We may have some great experiences in life – akin to the sugar and chocolate chips. But we also have a lot of mundane, or even things that are bad to the taste, so to speak. We go through times that are like eating a mouthful of flour. We encounter times that are like the searing heat of an oven. We don't always like the individual ingredients, but if we trust the baker, we know that it can actually turn out okay in the end. And that is the kind of long-term view we need to have of God and life. We don't always know why bad stuff happens, or why God allows certain things. But through it all, we know that we can trust Him – and that God can cause all things to work together for good. He can take the good and the bad and the intense experiences of our lives, and actually mix them around for our good and growth if we allow Him.

Earlier we looked briefly at the story of Joseph and how he learned to forgive. But that change of heart developed only after years of heartache and years in the furnace of affliction. You see, when he was younger, Joseph was given a dream by God – he saw himself as a leader among his family. His siblings, even his parents, were bowing down to him and he was ruling over them (Genesis 37:5-11). Rather foolishly, he told everyone his dream and the result was that his brothers resented his arrogance and privilege.

Maybe after receiving those dreams Joseph thought God would somehow make him rich and famous, or that everyone would recognize God's hand on his life. But his dreams, instead of causing everyone to be amazed, had the opposite effect – they stirred up jealousy and hatred instead.

So rather than an easy path to leadership, Joseph found himself in a major detour. He was emotionally and physically abused by his brothers – thrown into a pit and then sold as a slave into forced labor. And then, as we noted earlier, when he did eventually start climbing the ranks of leadership he ended up in prison on false charges. His dreams were once again collapsing all around him.

Joseph's "detour" lasted a long time. He was 17 when he was sold by his brothers (Genesis 37:2) and it wasn't until he was 30 years old that he was made ruler of Egypt (Genesis 41:46). That means he spent almost 13 years in servitude in a foreign land. But even then, his dreams had not been completely fulfilled – it would be another 9 years before his family came and bowed down to him, finally fulfilling the initial dreams he had. That's 22 years! Over two decades of hardship, inner turmoil, and of pain.

My point here is that God uses all the experiences of our lives, both the good and the bad and He alone can turn them into something of great worth and value. Those many "in-between" years that Joseph experienced were not wasted but were actually used to fashion him into the leader he needed to be. As we saw earlier, what was meant for bad can actually be turned into good (see Genesis 50:20).

It is never too late to see God-given dreams fulfilled. And it's never too late to begin again, or even to let Him into your life for the very first time!

## It's Not Too Late

This world is not our home, but it often takes us a long time to understand that truth. My father-in-law, Joseph Grieco, battled prostate cancer for seventeen years. He spent the last few months of that battle in Baycrest Palliative Care facility in Toronto. One day, a much younger man named Norman was admitted and placed in the same large room with my father-in-law. Dad Grieco was eighty-eight and Norman was around sixty. Norman looked so young that it almost seemed like they might have made a mistake—but he was dying of cancer. Dad and Norman shared good moments together, like Super Bowl Sunday when Norman came over to Dad Grieco's corner of the room where we watched the game while munching on snack food and cheering our team on. We did not know it at the time, but my father-in-law had less than four weeks left to live and Norman, less than seven weeks. That night we cheered, laughed and, of course, ate a good portion of real, "healthy" food, forgetting for a while just where we were. But cancer is a relentless foe, and soon it became evident Dad Grieco would not be with us much longer, as that terrible disease continued to ravage his body.

He passed away peacefully on March 6, with family by his side. An hour later, I went over to tell Norman.

"Norman, are you still awake?"

"Yes," he answered.

I went behind his curtain. "My father-in-law just passed away a little while ago, and now he is with the Lord he loved."

Norman said simply, "I wish I could have that kind of hope."

We had never spoken of spiritual things before, so I decided to take this opportunity.

"You can," I replied.

He thought for a moment. "Well, I've never murdered anyone and I'm not that bad a person, though the crowd I ran with at the racetracks was pretty rough and their language wasn't good."

I explained to him that it was not about being good or bad. "The truth is, we're all lost, we're all messed up, and we need a Savior." I told Norman, that no matter how many good things we do, we cannot earn brownie points with God. Forgiveness is a gift that can only be given to us by Jesus through His death on the cross. "The blood Jesus shed cleanses us of our sins. But He is a gentleman and will not force His way on anyone. He waits for us to give Him permission to come in and be part of our life. And when we do, He comes into our hearts and gives us the gift of eternal life. That's what my father-in-law has; that's why he's in heaven now. Our part is to acknowledge we need Jesus, seek His forgiveness, and invite Him into our hearts. He then gives to us that forgiveness and the gift of eternal life. Would you like to pray to receive that, Norm?"

Norman nodded. "Yes, but I don't know how to pray. I've never really prayed before."

I asked him if he wanted me to lead him in a prayer of forgiveness, so he could ask Jesus into his life, and Norman agreed. And so, we prayed. At one point in the prayer, I began, "Lord, forgive me for hurting others," to which Norm added, "Yes, please forgive me for hurting others, I know I have." I continued, "And Lord, forgive me for hurting myself," and Norm prayed, "Yes, forgive me for hurting myself." I went on, "And Lord, forgive me for hurting You." At this point Norman cried out, "Yes, oh God, please forgive me for hurting You! I've hurt You the most!" Tears were streaming down his face as he prayed those words. Then he invited Jesus into his life as Saviour and Lord.

> **It's never too late for God to give you a second chance!**

When we had finished, he said, "It's a miracle. I feel so much peace."

"Norman, that's the presence of Jesus in your heart now," I responded. "He is real, and He has given you the gift of eternal life."

Norman hugged me. "Thank you! Thank you!"

Indeed, it was a miracle for a man like Norman, who was not religious and who had not given God much thought his whole life, to discover the mercy and grace of God near the end of his journey. Two days later, when I was visiting Norman before my father-in-law's wake, he said, "Paul, I don't think I'll be here much longer. Will you do my funeral?"

"Yes, I would be honored," I said.

Norman passed away exactly three weeks after my father-in-law died, on March 27. He is now with the Lord.

When we realize it is never too late for God, and when we give Him our painful experiences, He can use it for good. It's never too late for Him to give you a second chance. He can make all things beautiful in His time.

### Rest and Redirection

After 9 years of running *Nite Lite Live,* I entered another season of ministry. But it did not start the way I had wanted. The years of working through the night (2:00-4:30 am) took its toll and I began to experience what my doctor said was *burnout*.

While part of the issue was the stress of the schedule, the other aspect was that I had always found it hard to say 'no' and to set boundaries. After working all night, I would also work much of the next day, calling back many of the people who had prayed on the program the night before. I was burning the candle at both ends, as they say, and eventually it wore me down.

God gives us boundaries for a reason. He set aside a Sabbath as a boundary for the work week. As important as all the other needs, events, and business activities were, His people needed to learn to make time to rest and be in His presence.

Jesus, while ministering to the needs around Him, knew how to say no. One time after a great night of ministry the crowds came surging around him, but Jesus told the disciples, "let's go somewhere else" (Mark 1:37-38). On another occasion, after a draining time of ministry coupled with the difficult news that his cousin John the Baptist had been murdered, Jesus said to the disciples, "Let's go off by ourselves to a quiet place and rest awhile" (Mark 6:31, NLT). There is a balance that we need in life, of giving and receiving. If you are empty and drained emotionally, it is very difficult to minister to those in need. God's word encourages us to be wise and to take time to be in God's presence, time to rejuvenate, so we can have the energy and strength we need to minister His compassion to others as well.

Aren't you glad that God gives us grace? We keep learning, we keep growing. We never arrive at a place where we know everything or have life figured out perfectly!

I needed to take some prolonged time off. As I did, not only did the Lord refresh me, he also opened my eyes once again to the needs of some of the most desperate people in the world.

# Further Reflection

*"At the time I have decided, my words will come true. You can trust what I say about the future. It may take a long time, but keep on waiting – it will happen!" (Habakkuk 2:3, CEV)*

1. Are there dreams that God has given you that have yet to see fulfillment?
2. Do you find it hard to establish boundaries in your life?
3. Do you make time with God a priority?

### *"It is never too late to begin again!"*

Go to **www.DontWasteYourPain.com/book** or scan the code on the right for videos and other resources related to this chapter!

# Chapter 13: Don't Waste Your Pain!

God does not want us to waste our pain! In other words, God wants to do something with your pain and mine. He wants to build a bridge with it over which we can walk into the lives of other broken people, so that the grace we receive from Jesus, our wounded healer, becomes the grace that we give to others who are broken.

Usually, we speak of an object being wasted *when it is something valuable*. We can waste time or money, or someone can waste their talent or an opportunity. Usually, it is something that is appreciated or has some kind of worth or potential.

So why do we speak of pain in this way? Because there is actually some value in pain, as Dr. Brand earlier showed. Whether we like it or not, part of our life has been invested in that painful experience. *It has cost us time and tears, sleepless nights, and anxious days*. While the experience has been hurtful, overwhelming, crushing at times, it also has the potential to be redeemed into something greater. When we bring it to God, He takes those tears, those experiences, and He transforms them

> **Your pain has cost you something, therefore it is valuable. Don't waste it!**

into something of worth. Those sleepless nights are not wasted. Those prayers and tears are not wasted. The wounds you carry with you can be turned around to bring healing to others. Just as the wounds of Jesus bring healing, so – in a much more limited sense – our wounds can be conduits of healing and hope to others. And as God's love pours through us to others the amazing thing is that we ourselves also experience greater joy and healing than we thought possible!

You have learned so much on your journey of pain, you have shed many tears, and you can relate to so many others. Do not waste that. Let God use it for something positive!

Like the diamond that is precious because of the pressure it has experienced, your pain has given you greater value, greater purpose, and potentially greater impact.

## Pain and Purpose

Here are a few reasons why we encourage you not to waste your pain:

*You've made it through the pain* (or are presently making it through!) You've become stronger, you've grown wiser. Do not let the memories hold you back, or keep you bound to those past events. You can be set free through Jesus' grace and help!

*You've learned something* from those painful situations. Those lessons are valuable.

*You've been changed* by those circumstances. You're a different person than you were before. You can either change negatively, becoming bitter and angry, or you can change for the better. With God's help, becoming a person that can be a channel of His love and grace to others who are also in need.

*You have something to offer others* because of what you went through. In fact, someone needs your empathy, your wisdom, and your experience.

*You are valuable to God* and to this world. Jesus went through great pain for you, as well. You are therefore of great value to Him! Part of the way that His pain is not wasted is when you walk in the freedom He bought!

*So we say, "Don't Waste Your Pain!*

While I could never know the pain that you have been through, I have walked my own journey of pain, as I have shared in this book. I know from personal experience that God can redeem our hurts and our pain: the abuse, the disappointments, and the rejection. Our journey often takes twists and turns that we never wanted or hoped for. But as we look to the Lord for strength each day, He can give us new hope and new purpose. As we saw earlier, our past does not have to determine our future!

Allow me to summarize how I found healing and how each of us can find new purpose in life. I began to find purpose when I did the following:

- Decided to trust Jesus with my future
- Believed Jesus could use me despite my brokenness
- Stopped hiding my pain
- Learned to forgive
- Continued learning from my mistakes
- Was willing to see my brokenness as something God had equipped me with to bring healing to others
- Learned to look beyond myself

## Binding Up The Brokenhearted

One of the things that I have begun to realize is that because of my pain I can now deeply feel the pain of others and have a real compassion for those going through hurts. I have also learned that if I just focus on my own pain, turning inwards, I'm not fulfilling my full potential. In fact, I found great freedom – and even joy – as I discovered how I can help others overcome their pain. There are so many today who are hurting and wounded and need people who understand what they are going through and are willing to walk alongside them and help "bind up the brokenhearted."

After my time of rest and renewal mentioned in the last chapter, I joined a ministry raising awareness of the plight of Dalits and the marginalized in India.[35] Although Gloria and I had lived in India for a number of years, even then I was not fully aware of how deep-rooted the caste system was, or how the Dalits were so brutally treated.

Dalit literally means "one who is broken or crushed." They are considered "untouchable," deemed nonhuman, and worth even less than animals – they are outcastes. Just a quick search online for violence against Dalits will result in an appalling number of headlines: Dalits killed for going to the bathroom or eating in the presence of an upper-caste person.

## Meet Akshara

The very first time I met Akshara (not her real name), she wept as she told the story of how her mother had given her up to be a temple prostitute when she was just a little girl. She had been "offered to the gods" as a *devadasi* at the young age of five.

Akshara had begged her mother not to take her to the Hindu Temple that day for she knew all too well what it meant. She had heard the story of how her grandparents had also taken her mother to the temple for such a "dedication." She had seen many men mistreat her mother and watched her mother cry endless tears. Though she was very young, Akshara knew she did not want her life to look the same. But that day, mother and daughter kept walking until they reached the temple, where the Hindu priest performed the ceremony. There, her life was offered to the gods, and the priest gave her a necklace to set her apart from other people. The necklace was beautiful—but young Akshara had no idea of the horror and sexual abuse that would be inflicted upon her by the time she was twelve.

As if being a Dalit was not bad enough, Akshara was forced that day to become a *Devadasi*. However, it was not until she entered puberty that the full consequences of her mother's decision struck Akshara with piercing pain. The Hindu priest drugged her the first few times she was sexually abused in order to break resistance. Soon thereafter, she became pregnant. She was not yet a teenager and barely understood what was happening to her own body, let alone her soul.

Tragically, Akshara's story was not an isolated one. It opened my eyes to the greatest case of human enslavement on our planet, that of the Dalits of India. It seems impossible that such atrocities could be happening in the twenty-first century.

That first day we talked, she had brought with her six other former *devadasi*, all of whom were willing to share their stories. The women said that many *devadasi* ended up contracting HIV and were tossed aside to die, their children left alone to struggle for survival. In fact, just three weeks earlier, Akshara's sister, also a *devadasi*, had died of AIDS leaving behind two teenage children.

As Akshara grew older, often she would be used fifteen to twenty-five times in one day by different men. The pain was so terrible and many times over the years she just wanted to die. But then something happened – in her twenties she met Jesus. Akshara's tears flowed freely as she shared this turning point in her story.

Akshara now lived in the village with her mother and grandparents. Their home was simple with walls of mud and cow dung, painted on the outside in bright-blue paint and on the inside in a natural earth color. The kitchen, a small room with pots and an open fire where they cooked their meals, was filled with smoke as Akshara shared more of her story. Holes in the walls allowed sunlight to streak inside, symbolic of the light of Jesus that had broken through the darkness to shine into Akshara's life.

It was unimaginable to me that her grandparents had offered their daughter, Akshara's mother, to the temple priests so many years before. The cruel cycle had continued with Akshara and her sister bearing this same dehumanizing abuse. At one point, I asked her mother why she had given her daughters as a *devadasi*? She cried and said, "I don't know. I just didn't know better. There was nothing else I could do." I asked if she had ever apologized to Akshara for giving her a life of terrible physical and emotional pain. When she said that she had not, I asked whether she would like to. Through tears, Akshara's mother asked forgiveness from her daughter, and Akshara also in tears, received her mother's apology. To see Akshara forgive her mother was very moving, and it magnified for me just how far God's grace can reach. It reminded me of Isaiah 1:18: "Though your sins are like scarlet, they shall be as white as snow; though they are red as crimson, they shall be like wool."

As I pondered all that I was hearing, I wondered why the West knew so little of the terrible plight of these women? Why did the church know so little about it? Thankfully, there were people working tirelessly to help free women like Akshara. Still, I felt deep sorrow for her and the thousands of other women like her who were forced to endure years of heinous abuse. In my journal that night I wrote these words:

> The depth and degree of the pain—emotional, mental, physical, spiritual, and every other kind—of the Dalits is almost beyond comprehension. They are treated as subhuman and at every level of life they face unbelievable discrimination. I am only now beginning to see on a personal level that these are real people. The more I read, see, and hear, the more overwhelming it is. I knelt by my bed and wept. Something must be done to help them. Lord, help me to do something!

**Finding Purpose**

I believe that I have found my purpose in life - by *doing something* to bring freedom to others bound in the cycle of pain, abuse, suffering, and sorrow. My purpose is bigger than just me! It is greater than just my own comfort.

Unlike so many others, Akshara's story has a positive ending. She went from being a Devadasi who was humiliated and debased many times each day, to a health care worker assisting other Devadasis with the tools and knowledge they needed to live a healthy life and care for their personal safety. Alongside this, Akshara would also share about the person of Jesus and how Jesus had changed her life and had given her meaning, purpose, and self-worth. Not only had the cycle of pain been broken, but a new cycle had begun – one of hope and healing!

The wonderful fact is that the more we allow God to use us as a conduit of healing, the more healing we ourselves receive. The words of Jesus that "it is more blessed to give than to receive" (Acts 20:35) are true in so many areas of life. It is by coming to recognize the great need around me, learning to reach out and bring healing to others, that has brought such joy to my soul!

I encourage you to take that next step – as you receive healing for the hurts you have experienced, look beyond yourself and see how you can bring hope and restoration to others. It may be something very simple, it might be something radical. Ask God to begin to guide you and lead you to the "right place at the right time" so you can bring His love and freedom to others as well. I want to leave you with three simple thoughts:

> **Your purpose is bigger than you!**

**Look upward** – to God. There is hope. God cares for you. God can use you! Your past does not determine your future!

**Look inward** – what are you holding on to? Hiding from? Are you harbouring unforgiveness? What has your season of pain taught you?

**Look outward** – who can you serve? What area of injustice can you bring God's hope to? Is there a way you can use your pain to bring life and healing to others?

## Conclusion

As I look back now at myself as a seven-year-old boy sitting in front of the black-and-white television watching *Gunsmoke*, my heart breaking at the suffering of others as my brothers laughed, I realize that it does not matter where in the world I have traveled, whether it be from a small-town church in rural Ontario to late-night television sets across Canada to mud huts in the villages of Africa or the megacities of India. In the end, I always come back to

God's heart for the hurting that allows even a child to sense the pain of others and to suffer with them

Over the years, I began to understand that the Lord Jesus is able to redeem our pain if we let Him. No matter where I traveled, my own brokenness became one of my greatest resources in ministering to others. As we saw earlier, this is what the Lord himself spoke of when He told the apostle Paul "my power is made perfect in weakness" (1 Corinthians 12:8).

No longer do we need to fear our weakness, for this can be the place where God's power flows through us. In a very real sense, Christ's power rests on us in such weakness. Rather than living in arrogance, we are humbled when broken. As a result, God's power has a chance to flow to us and then through us. Remember, it's not shameful to be broken, we all are.

The words of this scripture are beautiful to me because they reinforce the key thought of this book: the Lord will not waste our pain if we give it to Him. In time, He will use what we have been through to build a bridge over which we can walk into the lives of others who are broken so that the grace we have received becomes the grace we can give in the power of Christ. Do not be afraid to tell your story and ask God to lead you to people who are hurting. As you share, be patient with people; remember how long it took you to recover. If you ever doubt this, return to the stories of redemption in this book—the stories of Akshara, Francis, Margaret, and others. Determine to become a wounded healer, like each of them, and like Jesus! Never forget that your story, no matter how tragic, is redeemable. No matter how broken you may feel, remember that what the enemy of our soul means for evil, God has meant for good (Genesis 50:20). **Don't Waste Your Pain**!

# Further Reflection

*"We can rejoice, too, when we run into problems and trials, for we know that they help us develop endurance. And endurance develops strength of character, and character strengthens our confident hope of salvation. And this hope will not lead to disappointment. For we know how dearly God loves us, because he has given us the Holy Spirit to fill our hearts with his love."* (Romans 5:3-5, NLT)

1. Why does God want you to not waste your pain? What can happen if you allow Him to transform it?

2. Can you think of something of value that you have learned through your pain?

3. Reflect for a moment on the pain that others around you are going through. Are there ways that the lessons you have learned can help bring healing to others?

4. According to Paul in Romans 5:1-5, what does suffering lead to? How has this been your experience?

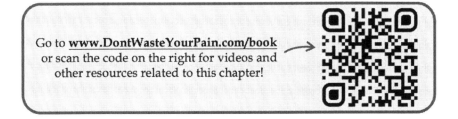

Go to **www.DontWasteYourPain.com/book** or scan the code on the right for videos and other resources related to this chapter!

If you have never asked Jesus to forgive you of your sins, and start you on the path of true healing, I encourage you to pray the prayer below:

> *Dear Jesus, please take my life and make it what you want it to be. I surrender it to you as my Lord. Please forgive my sins and show me how to find your purpose for my life. Thank you for dying for me on the cross. I receive you as my Savior. Lord I give you all the pain and hurt from my past. Please take it and turn it into a great blessing for me and for others. Amen.*

---

**If you've prayed this prayer, of if you want to have someone pray with you, why don't you call Crossroad's 24/7 prayer line. It's free and they'd love to hear from you:**

**1-866-273-4444.**

# STEPS TO HEALING
(Condensed from chapter 4)

*Here are a few steps that will help us face the pain of our past, and move into a place of wholeness.*

1. **If there is abuse happening right now,** you need to see how you can remove yourself from that situation.
2. **Cry out to God.** He really is on our side, and He can give us the supernatural strength and wisdom to deal with the pain of the past.
3. **Find someone to walk through the pain with you**. We need someone else's perspective and wisdom. This is where a counselor is so helpful. If you are not sure who to call, you can always call Crossroads as they have a 24/7 number you can call for prayer or to be connected to a church or counselor: 1-866-273-4444.
4. **Remember it takes time.** We need to understand that our pain has shaped us over time, and it will take time to bring healing as well.
5. **Take ownership of what you can**. We need to understand our "raw response." How do we react when we are raw, hurt, or have an emotional wound? Do we resort to any of the "fight, flight, or freeze" responses we looked at earlier?
6. **Take small steps.** Based on your talks with a counselor, with owning the things that you can control or change, set realistic goals. Do not expect everything to change overnight. But you can be persistent in taking a series of small steps that will help you eventually come to a place of wholeness.
7. **Look outward.** It is often as we begin to move beyond focusing on our own pain, to the pain of others, that we actually find healing for our own hurts!
8. **Believe**! Keep trusting that God wants your best and can help you.

# About the Author

Paul Willoughby is an ordained minister with the Pentecostal Assemblies of Canada. Since 1972 he has served as pastor, global worker, and as a Christian television host. His passion is to help the hurting, marginalized and forgotten, offering the hope and love that is found in Jesus Christ.

Get in touch with him at **www.dontwasteyourpain.com** or by sending an email to: **paul@dontwasteyourpain.com**

# NOTES

**CHAPTER 1**

1 Margaret Davidson, interview by Paul Willoughby. *Nite Lite Live* (April 2, 2008). Toronto: CTS.

2 Margaret Davidson, Blake Davidson, *Scars Don't Hurt: A story of triumph over sexual abuse*. (Florida: Creation House Press, 2004).

**CHAPTER 3**

3 See: www.merriam-webster.com/dictionary/broken accessed Dec 8, 2019.

4 https://overcomingabuse.org/

5 See "Child of Woe movie" on youtube.

6 C. S. Lewis, *The Problem of Pain* (New York: Macmillan, 1962), 93.

**CHAPTER 4**

7 Paul David Tripp, *Suffering: Gospel Hope When Life Doesn't Make Sense* (Wheaton, IL: Crossway, 2018), 27.

8 Emerge Ministries. Web: https://emerge.org/services phone: 800-621-5207 email: info@emerge.org

9 Strong's number 1977.
See: https://www.billmounce.com/greek-dictionary/epiripto

10 Dr Dobbins used to say this often. For more on his life and ministry see Emerge Ministries: www.emerge.org

**CHAPTER 5**

11 This is a phrase I first heard when I read chapter 3 of David Seamands book "*Healing for Damaged Emotions*" (Colorado Springs: David Cook, 1981). I believe it was initially popularized by Henri Nouwen in his book "*Wounded Healer*" (New York: Doubleday, 1972).

12 Philip Yancey, *Grace Notes: Daily Readings with Philip Yancey* (Grand Rapids: Zondervan, 2009), 225-226.

13 Richard Dobbins, "*Healing for the Hurts in Your Past*." (Emphasis mine). Accessed April 28, 2015. http://www.drdobbins.com/guidelines-for-great-living/articles/healing-for-the-hurts-in-your-past-part-one

14 Rebecca Rowan, *Healer*. Aired on 100 Huntley Street 1999, copyright with SOCAN 1999.

**CHAPTER 6**

15 Paul Brand and Philip Yancey: *The Gift of Pain* (Grand Rapids: Zondervan, 1993).

16 Brand & Yancey, *The Gift of Pain*, 3-5.

17 Brand & Yancey, *The Gift of Pain*, 13. Emphasis mine.

[18] See Mickey Robinson, "*Falling into Heaven*" (Racine: Broadstreet Publishing, 2014). Also see his website: www.mickeyrobinson.com.

[19] *Life is hard but God is good.* PAMELA THUM and JOEL LINDSEY. Copyright 1995 Paragon Music (ASCAP) (Administered by Brentwood-Benson Music Publishing, Inc.)

[20] Ajith Fernando, *The Call to Joy and Pain: Embracing Suffering in Your Ministry* (Wheaton: Crossway, 2007) 34.

## CHAPTER 8

[21] Oswald Chambers, *My Utmost for His Highest*, (Grand Rapids: Discovery House Publishers, 1992), Oct 17.

[22] See: http://www.100huntley.com/watch?id=226960&title=rev-billy-graham-on-canada--tribute-to-billy-graham

[23] Melody Green, *No Compromise* (Nashville: Thomas Nelson, 2008), 441.

[24] Ajith Fernando, *The Call to Joy and Pain: Embracing Suffering in Your Ministry* (Wheaton: Crossway, 2007), 31.

[25] Willoughby, Paul and Gloria, *Not My Own*. Written in Uganda 1982, copyright with SOCAN 1988.

## CHAPTER 10

[26] This quote has been attributed to Nelson Mandela and many others. However, it seems to have been popularized first of all by Alcoholics Anonymous.

[27] Corrie Ten Boom, *Tramp for the Lord* (Fort Washington: CLC Publications, 1974), 57.

[28] Lewis Smedes, *Forgive and Forget: Healing the Hurts We Do Not Deserve* (San Francisco: Harper, 1984), 133.

## CHAPTER 11

[29] Shingal, Ankur , "The Devadasi System: Temple Prostitution in India," UCLA Women's Law Journal, 22(1). 2015. https://escholarship.org/content/qt37z853br/qt37z853br.pdf

[30] Swami Harshananda, *All About Hindu Temples* (Madras: Sri Ramakrishna Math, 1991).

[31] Banarjee, Ruben. "Burning Shame." *India Today* (February 8, 1999).

[32] A movie was recently made about this tragic event: "The Least of These."

[33] E. Stanley Jones, *Christ of the Indian Road*, (Abingdon Press, 1925), 35.

[34] See: https://tressa.ca/

## CHAPTER 13

[35] Name withheld for security reasons

Manufactured by Amazon.ca
Bolton, ON